TABLE OF CONTENTS

Foreword

Here is a way to do what the church once did so well. Here is a way to preach from the whole liturgy. This is a way of preaching that is born out of the preacher's own love for the liturgy. Let's say a preacher recognizes how the liturgy as a whole and in each of its parts can gather up and give shape to the church, to the baptized people. Let's say a preacher knows it firsthand, has experienced how the singing and walking of a procession can offer us a way to see our whole life, every day after every day. Or a preacher has experienced how the posture of attentive standing and praying thankful words seeps into all standing, all moments to make them thankful.

Shouldn't a preacher find ways to preach this? Shouldn't a preacher be always ready to say: "Brothers and sisters, think about what we do when we clasp hands and say 'Christ's peace!' Or, 'Friends, let's reflect on what it is like to walk from the outside into this house of the church.' Or, 'Church, have you ever really bowed deeply? What was that like?'"

Probe the way that we pray when we pray well, and you will probe the whole of baptized life. This has nothing to do with "explaining" the liturgy. It is the opposite of trying to tell people what the liturgy "means." Here the preacher knows that the liturgy is what explains us. The liturgy tells us what we mean.

The kind of preaching offered in this book will help that happen. It presumes that a parish is making good efforts with its liturgy so that the gestures, objects, words and songs are worthy of our talk and reflection. The preacher helps to open the depths and the ambiguities of our rituals. The preacher recognizes that the rituals belong to the people, not to some elite. This way of preaching says: "Let us ponder these things together because each of us has something to bring to the others." The preacher asks more questions.

Finally, recognize how great is our need for this sort of preaching. If the liturgy is ever to show us baptized people how we are to walk and sing and talk and listen through our lives in this world, how we are to conduct ourselves and so become a gospel preached day by day, then we have to make that liturgy our own. That is exactly what begins to happen when we preach in this way.

Gabe Huck

OF SAVING SIGNS AND WONDROUS WORDS

Why do we burn incense in church? What does Alleluia mean? What's the significance of stretching out your arms when praying the Our Father? Why is Sunday chosen for Mass?

The short essays in this book invite you to think about some of the actions, words and objects that we use in worship, so that together the whole assembly of baptized people can fully, consciously and actively, always and everywhere, give God thanks and praise. Grace builds on nature, so the actions, words and objects that we use to worship God come from our ordinary experience: walking and singing, gathering around a dining room table, listening and speaking to each other in turn.

When we as the body of Christ do these actions, sing these words and handle these objects, the ordinary reveals the extraordinary, the human leads to the divine. And this divine-human encounter changes us, saves us. That is what the Second Vatican Council meant when it said, "In the liturgy, *by means of signs perceptible to the senses,* human sanctification is signified and brought about in ways proper to each of these signs" (*Constitution on the Sacred Liturgy,* 7).

So this book is an invitation, an excuse, a guide to ponder the beauty of 25 of the saving signs and wondrous words of our tradition.

How to Use This Book

You may want to read this book one chapter at a time, Sunday by Sunday before going to Mass. This book doesn't cover everything; no one book could. And the chapters aren't in any tight order, so you can look at the Table of Contents and read about the things that you wonder about most often.

You can also use this book to preach about the liturgy, whether you are an ordained preacher who gives homilies during Mass, or a minister who gives retreats, leads evenings of reflection, trains ministers, helps the newly baptized reflect on the mysteries, teaches children or preaches at daily prayer or other rites.

Preaching about the Liturgy

But aren't homilies supposed to be about the scriptures? Normally, yes. However, the *General Instruction of the Roman Missal* states:

> The homily is an integral part of the liturgy. . . . It is necessary for the nurturing of the Christian life. It should develop some point of the readings *or another text from the Ordinary or from the Proper of the Mass of the day,* and take into account the mystery being celebrated (41).

Sometimes it is helpful to preach about a wondrous word or phrase from the liturgy, or to unpack some of the rich meanings behind a gesture or a posture. Such preaching can stir people's hearts and encourage us all to sing the word, make the gesture or take the posture deliberately — with more reverence, joy and grace.

Although it's not helpful to try to force a connection between these words and scripture, many of these essays make scriptural allusions. So if you are introducing or nurturing the practice of evening prayer in the parish, and using Psalm 141, you might want to preach about incense (see page 67). Or on Pentecost, you might want to preach on how we call down the Holy Spirit on the gifts and the church in every eucharistic prayer (see page 35).

Most of these essays echo scriptural themes. And sometimes a word or phrase from the day's scripture suggests a homily on a particular word, gesture, posture or object used in the liturgy. For example, on Passion Sunday in Year A, the Gospel of Matthew includes Jesus' words: "All of you must drink from it, for this is my blood, the blood of the covenant." The church will likely be crowded, maybe with some folks who have been away for a time. What a great opportunity to preach about the importance of receiving from the cup (see page 52), and how drinking from the cup is necessary if we are to follow Jesus from the table to the cross to the tomb and beyond.

For more help discovering connections between these essays, the lectionary and the rites, see the appendix at the end of this book.

Preaching about elements of the liturgy need not be limited to Mass. If the new lectors are gathered, why not preach briefly on the significance of the ritual dialogue ("The word of the Lord. Thanks be to God.") in addition to explaining how to use the microphone? Or maybe the group that decorates the church and washes the altar linens might be interested to hear some words on why the altar is so important to our life in common.

Preparing to Preach

To be effective, a homily or reflection must be prepared thoroughly and then rehearsed. A strong help in preparing to preach is the U.S. bishops' document *Fulfilled in Your Hearing.* Please read or reread that document, and pay close attention to the suggested methods of preparation that it offers.

This book can help by giving you words with which to hold up a saving sign or wondrous word from our rites for the church to ponder. You can read right from this book, but practice enough so that your reading is lively and sincere, not rote and boring.

You will need to add your own words to these words. You will need to add some sentences that help these words make more sense to the particular people to whom you are preaching. Add examples from your parish's life. Include references to specific, recent events. But make sure that the words that you add dance rather than trudge along, evoke rather than explain.

Savoring and Wondering

The deeds that we do, the words that we use in our rites are like a film classic: They yield more meaning when they are observed carefully, then examined again. The deeds that we do, the words that we use are good wine: They taste better when they are sniffed and then held for a moment on the taste buds before being swallowed. May this book help you to savor the deeds, wonder at the words, and delight in the rites of our life in Christ.

ALLELUIA!

It is surely the angels' praise before God's throne—their unceasing song. Hebrew's *hallelujah* is Latin's *alleluia*—one word that deserves never to be muttered, always to be sung from our lips, whistled by the flute, broadcast by the drum, shouted with the trumpet's throat. Some would translate it as "Praise God," but how does one adequately translate a heartbeat or a head rush or a belly roar? The word itself is music: It sounds like what it means, resounding human joy that defies explanation. In the scriptures, it appears in only two places—in the Book of Psalms and in the Book of Revelation—always in song. *Hallelujah* begins and ends those psalms thought to be sung in the Temple's liturgies. And it is the triumphant refrain sung with "the voice of a great multitude, like the sound of many waters and like the sound of mighty thunderpeals crying out" at the end of the ages at the wedding feast of the Lamb (Revelation 19:6).

And so we, too, sing it—never merely *say* it—in our earthly liturgy, our little rehearsal for that day when Christ shall return, and we shall be made whole, and the cosmos will be healed, and God will be all in all. We sometimes sing it as a part of a hymn, and we always sing it (except during Lent) to greet the gospel. This has been the custom since the fourth century in North Africa. There was a tradition then for a soloist to elaborate the last vowel, the last "a," beyond the singing of

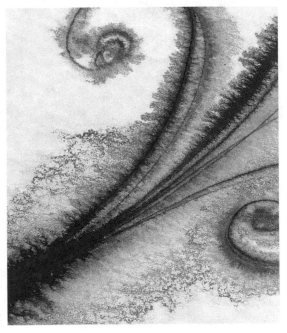

the assembly, as long as she or he could. It was as if the soloist didn't want to let go of this holy word, or end this holy song. In Latin, this prolonged singing of Alleluia's last syllable is called *jubilus;* Augustine called it "joy without words."

And that in fact is what it is: pure joy; joy beyond telling; joy at the prospect of hearing the gospel again this day, this hour in this assembly. Such joy propels us to our feet and shines like the candles carried, smells like perfumed clouds of incense swirling, dances above our heads like the book held aloft.

In the sober season of Lent, we hang up our joy like the dejected, exiled Israelites hung up their harps. We in the West fast from our holy song. We don't forget it, though, and we even begin to long for it. Then it becomes the song of Easter *par excellence,* the harbinger of the resurrection, the first notes of the melodious good news that a death has conquered death. And the Alleluia at the Vigil resonates in our humming and our hearts even longer than it reverberates in our hall.

If you listen to the earth returning to life these spring days, perhaps you will hear with your heart that it is the root note of every robin's song, the refrain of every breeze whispering through branches, the hymn of every seed case cracking open, every bud blooming. Walk by the lake. Do you hear the water chortle it, lapping up against the shore? If the sun could sing, it would sing Alleluia! If animal lips could form but one word, it would be Alleluia!

So Alleluia is not only a song for church, it is the universe's music. Hear it as the car whooshes down the street, as the train clanks into the station. Sing it syncopated as you jog. Bellow it in the shower with the water running. Chant it peacefully as you rock the baby to sleep or comb Grandma's gray hair. Breathe it out when you breathe your last: Alleluia!

Fifty days of rejoicing burst out of one word: Alleluia! Death dies, life lives in a song: Alleluia! Alleluia! Alleluia!

THIS ALTAR, THIS DINING TABLE

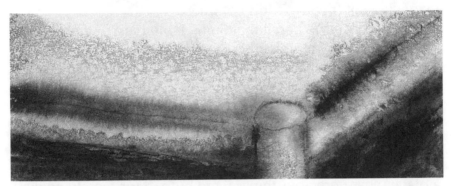

I don't know who made it, nor even exactly how old it is. I know that Rita's mom owned it first—probably for years, maybe even a generation. When her mom died, Rita gave it to Tim. When Tim moved out of his flat into a place that was already furnished, he lent it to me. Then hundreds of dinners were shared, five New Year's Eve parties celebrated and countless conversations held around that round, oak, pedestal table.

When I moved to a different city, the table went back to Tim. And for six years after that, whenever I came home for Thanksgiving or Christmas or a summer visit, dinner was shared around that table. Some of the friends who gathered there are gone: moved away, drifted away, two more (besides Rita's mom) now dead. Yet somehow, every holiday, more than just food was put on that table, and more than just the living sat around it. That's why last year, when Tim moved again and knew that he couldn't take the old oak table with him, I had to get it and bring it back to my house. We both knew that he couldn't just sell it like a used car. The table has a history, a memory. It is holy. It needed to be handed on carefully, to someone who knew and understood its importance, someone who would continue to invite others to gather around it, conscious of all who had gathered around it before.

A dining table is different from a couch or a dresser or even a coffee table. The continual gathering around a dining table, mostly for the sharing of meals but also for conversation and card games and the like, invests the table with a spirit, lends it a memory. Yes, more than just food is placed there, and more than just the living sit around it. Think of the dining table in your house, or in the house of your parents or grandparents or primary circle of friends. Is this not true?

It is most true about the dining table here in the house of the church. More than food is shared here. And more than just the living gather around it.

This dining table is an altar. The word "altar" comes from a Latin word that probably first meant "to burn up." In antiquity, the altar — more a barbecue pit than a dining table — was the place where blood was spilled, flesh was roasted, and incense, oil and grain were burned. The altar was a place of sacrifice — a place where precious things were burned (or merely cooked) in order to send them (or at least the smell of them roasting) "up" to the gods. And sometimes an ancient altar was a place where people ate with their gods: The smoke of roasted lamb or goat was sent up to heaven. Being spirits, the gods "ate" delicious smells. The roasted flesh (no use wasting it!) sometimes was distributed among the people, who, being bodies as well as souls, gladly ate it.

The Christian altar, too, is a place for sacrifice and a place for eating and drinking with God but in a much different way. The Living God does not need barbecue smells, and in fact, all such sacrifice is now obsolete. The Living God does not desire us to burn up precious things, for the most precious sacrifice of all already has been offered up and accepted.

Jesus' self-sacrificing love turned the cross into the ultimate altar: the place of offering, the place to find God. Because of the cross, we no longer have to spill blood or stoke destructive fires. Because of the cross, the Christian altar is no longer the blazing pit or the executioner's weapon. The Living God's altar has become a dining table, our sacrifice, the lifting up of our hearts, the sharing of Christ's paschal meal.

This is God's desire for us: that death be turned into life and that love be forever. This is what Jesus worked for and longed to reveal to us. This is why Jesus sat down at so many dining room tables to eat and drink with sinners, so that they could eat and drink with God and be made whole. Think of all the meals that Jesus shared: lunch at Levi's house, supper at Simon's, the banquet at Bethsaida, meals with Martha and Mary, Sabbath dinner with a leader of the Pharisees, and the hospitality that Zacchaeus showed. Think of all those dining room tables!

So is it any wonder? When Jesus was being stalked by the secret police just hours before he was arrested, tortured, given the death penalty and killed, even on the threshold of all that, he sat down at the dining table in the cenacle to give us his body and his blood, his life and his love, broken in bread and poured out in wine.

Now God calls us to gather around this dining-table-turned-altar. And it's *our* lives lived in common, with and for each other, that God desires be placed on this table under the signs of bread and wine. And it's *our* hearts — our very selves — that God longs for us to lift up at this altar. We give to God our hearts — baked into this bread. We give our lives — all the pain and promise, joys and griefs wrung from them like this wine crushed from grapes. We put all that on this table, and God accepts it and makes it holy and gives it back to us as the body and the blood of Christ. The bread, the wine, *we* — the world — all of this is changed here.

More than food is put on this table, and more than we who live now gather around it. The body of Christ is not only on this table; the body of Christ is also *at* this table. Ringing round us at this table are the members of this parish who once worshiped here and who have gone before us in death. And ringing round us at this table are the saints whose hearts are lifted up to God. And ringing round us at this table are the martyrs, ancient like Agnes and recent like Romero, who gave their lives in perfect imitation of Christ, their bones broken like bread and their blood spilled out like wine.

And even though all these surround us at this altar, there is still room for more. There is still room for the members of this parish who aren't born or reborn yet. There is still room for the people in this neighborhood that we've yet to invite inside. There is still room for immigrants and migrants, for strangers and aliens, for people with whom we disagree and for others whom we dislike, for people who are different from us, and for people who sin just like us. Are we ready to welcome them to this table as we have been welcomed?

If we are, then the disagreements and discord that we may bring to this table will be healed. If we are, then our pains will be soothed, our problems solved and our joy will be magnified a thousand times, so that peace might break out everywhere. For to come to this table is to come to Christ.

For that is finally what we name this table: Christ. On the day of its dedication, the bishop sprinkled this table with water, slathered it with a mixture of olive oil and perfume called chrism, robed it in fine linen and set lit candles around it. Sound familiar? We, too, on the day of our baptism were washed with water, anointed with oil, robed in fine garments and entrusted with the light — made into Christians, other Christs, altars of sacrifice and banquet tables for the hungry and the thirsty. This consecrated table, this altar stands here, Christ in our midst, the center of our life, our life lived for the sake of the world.

So we bow to this altar when we enter this room, and we bow again before we depart — not just a nod of the head but a slow, deep bow. And the priest and the deacon — and perhaps on some occasions all of us — kiss this altar when we approach it, embracing it in love.

These are prayers of the whole body, wordless gestures of profound power. The bow and the kiss are not only ways to show our respect for Christ in our midst, but these signs actually deepen that respect. The bow and the kiss are how we acknowledge and celebrate and believe in what happens at this altar of sacrifice, this paschal banquet table. The bow and the kiss signify our faith in the one to whom this table points, the one who on this table rests, the one who at this table stands, the one to whom this table, this altar draws us: Christ the sacrifice! Christ the meal! Christ the altar! Christ the banquet table of Easter-eternity!

I WILL BOW AND BE SIMPLE

We're proud of ourselves when we stand tall. When we are first able to pick our heavily diapered bottom off the ground and stand erect, however wobbly, we're happy, and we meet with cries of excited joy. Maybe in that instant we recall dimly that time before memory when the first man and the first woman straightened their backs and stiffened their necks to rise upright. And who hasn't felt right when he or she has stood up for something believed deeply, stood firm against something unjust?

Standing tall in these ways is an accomplishment of which to be proud, a stature for which to be grateful. And yet listen to what the Shakers sang in the nineteenth century:

I will bow and be simple, I will bow and be free.
I will bow and be humble, yea,
   bow like a willow tree.
I will bow, this is the token; I will wear the easy yoke.
I will bow and will be broken, yea,
   I'll fall upon the rock.

Once we have learned to stand tall, we must learn to bow as well. Or perhaps it is more precisely this: Once we learn how to truly bow down we know truly how to stand tall.

In the liturgy, we bow to the table, we bow at words in the creed and at the names of God, we bow to each other, and we bow to bread that is body and to the cup of wine that is blood. Why?

When we enter this room, and before we depart, we bow to this table. For us this table is Christ. Baptized in the Jordan by John, Jesus rose from the water, and the heavens opened to pour down Spirit on his body like so much fine ointment. And he was robed in light. Just like Christ, just like each of us in our own baptism, on the day of its dedication this beautiful table was washed in water, anointed with chrism, robed in fine linen, surrounded with lit candles. This table, this altar is Christ standing forever in our midst, calling us together, offering us a place. Christ is not only the sacrifice but also the altar, not only the meal but also the table.

And so we bow to this table. Wordlessly we admit our dependence on it. With our bodies we revere it. By bowing to this table, we pledge our lives to its purposes. We consent to share this meal of bread broken and wine poured out in order to become for others the sacrifice that we receive. "I will bow and will be broken, yea, I'll fall upon the rock."

And we bow at words. We bow at the words "who was born of the Virgin Mary and became one of us." We bow both to remember and to revere. We bow to remember (not just in our heads but in our bodies) that Jesus, Light from Light, became one of us and is God embodied. We bow to revere and respect the great mystery of incarnation, the great mystery of sacred bone and blood and breath, of humanity charged with divinity, and divinity enfleshed in matter. We bow at these words to remember and to revere the moment when God looked with love at creation and bowed down, rising up in human form to stand tall as the Savior.

We bow, too, at the names of God. At daily prayer, when each psalm is concluded with the doxology, we bow at the name of Father, Son and Holy Spirit. And some among us remember being taught to bow (our heads at least) at the name of Jesus, the name that means "God saves," the name that saves us. The nuns taught us to heed Saint Paul, who was quoting a favorite hymn when he reminded the church that at the name of Jesus, every knee must bow in the heavens, on earth and under the earth, and every tongue proclaim that Jesus Christ is Lord. So we bow at the holy name to put ourselves in right relationship: The name saves us, we are saved by the name. "I will bow, this is the token; I will wear the easy yoke."

We also bow to each other on occasion — when a minister incenses us, or we bow to the bishop who, as head of the church, represents the church. Some of our Asian sisters and brothers bow to give the kiss of peace — handshaking is not in their cultural repertoire. Without a word we admit our dependence on

each other. With our bodies we revere each other as Christians — as other Christs. We acknowledge, too, that because of Jesus, each of us is an icon of God, an image — however distorted or bent — of the divine. We revere the presence of God in each living tabernacle of flesh, and know — because Christ taught us so — that before we can approach God in sacrifice and in the supper, we must put down our gifts, bow to each other's needs and be reconciled to each other by a love that admits that it is in each other that we find God. "I will bow and be humble, yea, bow like a willow tree."

And finally we may bow to the bread that is body and the cup of wine that is blood. The *General Instruction of the Roman Missal* suggests that we show some sign of reverence for the holy food and drink that we are about to share. And so, before the minister of communion greets us, we bow. We bow low so that God — in the miracle that is a morsel and a sip — can raise us up, nourished, united to each other and united in Christ. We bow down because the wood of the oppressor's cross bowed down Jesus' back; we bow down so that as with Jesus, God may raise us up to a new life lived forever for others. "I will bow and be simple, I will bow and be free."

How do we bow? Standing up straight, arms at our sides or maybe crossed over the chest, muscles relaxed, breathing deeply, we bend at the waist until the upper half of our body is parallel to the ground. We bend slowly, gracefully, without looking up. Bent over, we pause for a moment, lingering in the precarious, compromised position in which we have placed ourselves. Then, just as slowly and gracefully as we descended, we rise, to stand upright again and face the object of our bow, faces flushed, muscles stretched, souls supple, hearts in the right place.

Bowing is more than a ritual gesture. It is a way of learning how to live in right relationship with the mystery that surrounds us, pervades us. If we bow down in awe and true humility and gratitude, then God will raise us up in wonder and in joy. An old brittle oak tree will break in a strong wind, but a supple pine or birch will bow before the gale in order to stand tall again in the breeze. And when the circumstances of our daily living oppress us and double us over and threaten to break our backs, we rely on the agility that bowing before God affords us. Bowing down and being raised up becomes the movement of living and dying and living anew. That's why Robert Frost could write about learning from swinging on limber birch trees how to bow and how to stand straight:

> It's when I'm weary of considerations,
> And life is too much like a pathless wood
> Where your face burns and tickles with the cobwebs
> Broken across it, and one eye is weeping
> From a twig's having lashed across it open.
> I'd like to get away from earth awhile
> And then come back to it and begin over.
> May no fate willingly misunderstand me
> And half grant what I wish and snatch me away
> Not to return. Earth's the right place for love:
> I don't know where it's likely to go better.
> I'd like to go by climbing a birch tree,
> And climb black branches up a snow-white trunk
> Toward heaven, till the tree could bear no more,
> But dipped its top and set me down again.
> That would be good both going and coming back.

DAY OF THE LORD, DAY OF THE CHURCH

Why *this* day for our assembling? Why this day for eucharist? Why Sunday?

Some say that the third commandment of the Law compels us to be here. But *Saturday* is the Sabbath, and that we Christians indeed have an obligation to worship on Sunday does not change that fact. Sunday is not the Christian Sabbath, the day of rest. It is something else.

The most obvious reason that we assemble on Sunday for eucharist is that this is the day that Christ rose from the dead. And we know from our history that Christians have gathered on Sunday for the word and the sacrificial meal from the beginning, even before one Sunday a year was kept as "Easter." That Sunday, the day of resurrection is certainly one of the primary reasons that we gather on this holy day. But as is always the case with God, there is more.

Before there were days, in the time before time, divine love overflowed and God said: "Let there be light!" So Sunday is the *first* day, the day when the Creator began creating, separating the light from the darkness. Sunday is the day of beginning, the day of light-separated-from-darkness, the day when God first looked at creation and called it good.

What better day to see Christ rise? So the first day is also the *third* day, the day on which Christ rose from the dead. And on the third day, Magdalene and her two companions — a trinity of women — came to know God as savior and redeemer. For when they went to the cemetery in the darkness before dawn, they were dazzled by the glory of a handsome angel and a neatly folded shroud in an otherwise empty tomb. That morning is brighter than all others since the beginning. And when the sun set that Sunday, while the apostles were huddled together shaking their heads in disbelief at what Magdalene had told them,

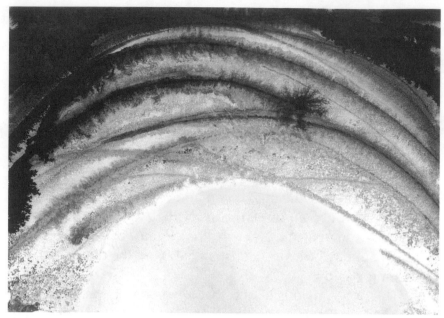

the risen Lord appeared in their midst (like a match struck in the dark) and said "Peace be with you." On Sunday, even dusk is redeemed, and nighttime made holy again. Sunday is the third day, the day when Christ rose from the dead and breathed peace. Sunday is the day of life-born-out-of-death.

Sunday is the day that the Holy Spirit came. According to the Gospel of John, it was on that first Easter evening that Jesus gave the Spirit. According to the Acts of the Apostles, it was 50 days after Easter — but still a Sunday — when wind shook the house and fire burned understanding into the brains of the apostles. They spilled into the streets of Jerusalem and preached so ferociously and with such joy that people thought they were drunk! Sunday is the day when the church began its mission. The first day is the *fiftieth* day — the day after seven weeks of seven days when all things come around full circle. The day of creation is the day of re-creation; the day when Christ rose is the day that the Spirit descended.

Because Sunday was the day when God began creating, when Jesus rose from the dead and when the Spirit descended, the early church began to call Sunday "the Day of the Lord," or "Lord's Day." In fact, later languages would capture this title: What we call "Sunday" in English — after an old, pagan way of reckoning the days after the planets — the Spanish call *Domingo* and the French call *Dimanche,* both meaning "Lord's Day."

For our ancestors, the name "Day of the Lord" had deep meaning. The "Day of the Lord" was the biblical name given by the prophets to the last day, the end of time when the Living God would appear on earth to work justice for the poor. The early church came to interpret the last day as the day Christ would return in glory and judge the living and the dead. So for the church, the first day, which is also the third day, which is also the fiftieth day, is most importantly the *eighth* day. Because there are only seven days in the week as we know it, the *eighth* day is a sign of eternity's dawn, the time beyond time, a rehearsal for the day that will last forever. Sunday is the day of heaven-on-earth and earth-becoming-heaven.

So, because Sunday means all of these things for we who are baptized and we who are preparing to be so changed, the Day of the Lord also is the Day of the Church, the day for us to be whom God calls us to be and to do what is most important to us: assemble, hear the word, intercede for the world, gather gifts for the poor and the church, give thanks and praise over bread and wine, and share in the body and the blood of Christ. And we do all of this *in here* to hasten that time *out there* when all people will be gathered in, called by name and welcomed; when all people will tell and hear the meaning of their lives and human history in ancient stories; when all people will have a seat at the table with God.

Read the Acts of the Apostles, where we first find Sunday called the Lord's Day. Notice all of the things that the church does on Sunday: There is eucharist, of course, but also baptism and the anointing and the laying on of hands. And there is preaching and healing and the doing of good works. Sunday is the day to be the church, the day to do what the church does.

According to the tradition at the time, the day began when the sun set the previous evening, so Sunday began at dusk on Saturday. At first, eucharist was celebrated after nightfall on Saturday. But eventually, evening meetings of all sorts were outlawed. The eucharist was moved to Sunday morning. In the Roman Empire, Sunday was a work day. Saturday — at least in

Jewish territories — was the day of rest; Sunday was business as usual. But for Christians, that business as usual was transformed because of the morning eucharist, and every task done on Sunday became an opportunity to bring the reign of God closer to completion.

Today, many of us again work on Sundays. This is unfortunate because it robs us of the leisure that we need to live differently this day, to dream about the world the way that it could be and to prepare ourselves to try again to make it so. But drawing on the experience of the first Christians, those of us who work this day can keep Sunday holy by dedicating our labor to the coming of God's reign. Practice finding God in signs of creation, resurrection and re-creation. Give thanks for God's goodness in the produce aisle of the market. Be Christ's healing hand in the nursing home. Hear the Spirit's coming as the laundry rustles on the clothesline, and smell the coming of the reign of God in bread rising in the oven. Breathe Christ's peace to those you encounter on your patrol.

For those of us who do not work on Sunday, let's resolve to keep the Day of the Lord and the Day of the Church as gracious stewards of holy time. Set the table at home with cloth and candles, and linger over a meal — taking turns with the preparation and clean-up! Listen to favorite music. Go to an art gallery. Play a game. But do these things differently today: Do them with others, or with another, perhaps someone who is lonely. Do them with gratitude in your heart and a prayer of praise on your lips.

Remember that this day is practice for eternity. And when it comes to an end, when the shift is over, the dinner dishes done, the sun set, lift up your hearts again to God, and give thanks and praise for this moment of heaven on earth and this promise of earth becoming heaven, this Sunday that God has given us.

THE WORD OF THE LORD. THANKS BE TO GOD!

It's such a brief conversation that we sometimes don't even hear ourselves engaged in it. "The word of the Lord," the reader says. "Thanks be to God!" we reply. "Good to see you." "Have a nice day." The danger of this ritual language is that it is so brief that we might miss its meaning. The delight of this ritual language is that it packs a punch: It captures rich and expansive truths in simple syllables. Turn the phrase over and you discover a map for navigating faith.

Of course, it's not simply the phrase, the words. It's also who says them, and when, and why. "The word of the Lord!" the reader says, at the conclusion of the reading. Sure, she is referring to what she has just proclaimed—the passage of scripture laid out for us in the book of readings, the lectionary. But when she—a baptized, anointed Christian—looks us—an assembly of the same—in the eyes and says this, she is saying more.

She is saying her name. *She* is the word of the Lord, the living, breathing utterance of God here and now, the lump of clay into which, with a word, God breathed life on the river bank in the garden. Taking the word of God in with her eyes and breathing it out with her voice, from her lips, *she* is the living proclamation of salvation, charged by Christ himself to go into the whole world to spread good news.

And she is saying *our* name. *We* are the word of the Lord, the resounding, thundering, echo of God's voice in this neighborhood, in this age, in this hour. Receiving the proclaimed word through our ears, we are pregnant with it. In us it gestates. It kicks at our insides and tumbles in our gut and struggles to be born—flesh of our flesh. It burns and it rips and it will not be held back.

By virtue of the baptism that we have received, we carry the word into the world. By virtue of this sacrificial meal that we share, we become this word for the world.

The scripture is the word of God. The lector is the word of God. The church is the word of God because Christ is the word of God: the word made flesh, the word in action, the word that calls us, the word that saves us, the word that sends us forth. So this thing that we do — this ritual action, in which two or three of us who have wrestled all week with the words of the book, climb this pulpit to proclaim this message as all of us eagerly and intently listen, and listen hard, and listen hard together — this ritual *action* is the word of the Lord. The living breathing word that is a dialogue, not a diatribe. A conversation, not a curse. A parable, not a platitude. A story, not a stipulation. For it is Christ himself who speaks when the scriptures are read in church.

The word of the Lord is Christ present in this assembly. And that word-made-flesh is active. It is the yeast that makes this bread, this people, rise. It is the yeast that ferments this water into a wine that quickens our spirit, frees our minds and loosens our tongues. This word creates: God said "Let there be . . . ," and there was, there is and there will be. This word saves: Jesus said, "This is my body broken for you. This is my blood poured out for you," and we are redeemed. This word lives: Christ says, "Receive the Holy Spirit," and we come out of our dumb tombs like so many Lazaruses, missionaries like Magdalene, preaching like Paul, talking with tongues we thought were glued to the roofs of our mouths, acting in ways we would have never imagined possible.

From this word we hurry to the supper. And from that banquet we go to a famished world. And there we listen for, we speak, the word of the Lord. Not in slick phrases or fancy words. Not necessarily with complete clarity. Maybe not even with talk at all. But with deeds. Deeds of dying and rising. Deeds of dying to self and rising to others, for others. From the supper to the world we are called. Called to listen for the word of God in human words. To speak the word of God in human terms. To love the word of the Lord. To live the word of the Lord. To be the word of the Lord.

How do we respond to such an invitation, to such a mystery? All words fail us except these: "Thanks be to God!" This is not our doing, not our reward, not even our just dessert. That we have ears to hear, a life to live, deeds to do—all this is pure grace. We would be speechless except to say, "Thanks be to God." And in so saying, mean "Yes, we will."

Yes, we will read this word, heed this word every day of our lives. Yes, we will love this word, live this word, be this word in the world, for the world. The word of the Lord! Yes! Thanks be to God! Thanks be to God!

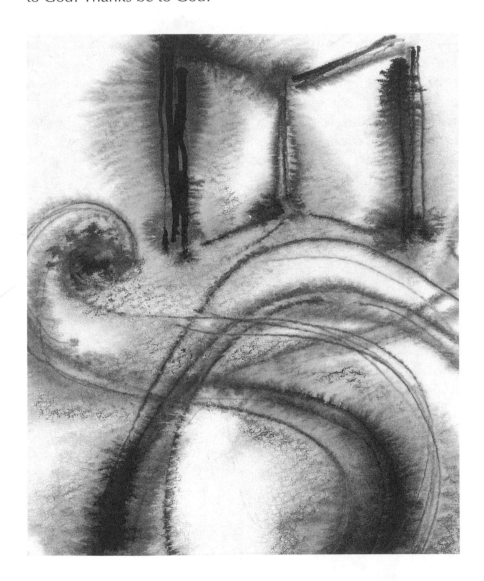

THE BODY OF CHRIST.
THE BLOOD OF CHRIST.
AMEN.

Have you ever been alone in a foreign place — or in a crowd of strangers — and heard your name called out? Even though you know that the person calling your name is not calling you but someone else with the same name, you cannot help but hear it and respond in some way: lifting your eyes, drawing a breath of anticipation, turning your head toward the voice. To be called by one's name is to be home.

And most of us have more than one name. Most of us have a first, a middle and at least one last name. Some of us have nicknames and pet names. Some of us have added "confirmation" names to the names we received at the font, and some of us have "names in religion" that we accepted when professing vows. When we love someone, there is no end to the names that we use: Honey, Love, My Sweet, Heart of My Heart.

So it is with God's people, the church. Jesus has called us by many names: Salt of the Earth, City on a Hill, Light to the Nations. And in the liturgy, the Spirit calls us by more intimate names. In the liturgy, the first name that the Spirit calls the church is "The word of the Lord." You may have thought that when the lector finishes the reading, looks at us and says "The word of the Lord," she is referring to what she just read. She is. But she also is looking us in the eyes when she says that, because in a sense, the church is the word of the Lord, spoken today, here, now. This is so because in Christ the word was made flesh, and in baptism our flesh is made word.

Wondrously, as if this is not endearment enough, we the church are called by holy names twice more. When we have lifted up our hearts, when we have given thanks and praise, when we have remembered how Christ loved us to the death and was raised up, when we have called down the Spirit, when we have broken the bread that is body and poured out into cups the wine that is blood, as we sing and come forward, all of us and each of us hears our two names spoken again: "The body of Christ. The blood of Christ."

Think of it! It is not only the consecrated bread to which the minister refers when she says to you, "The body of Christ." It is that and more. (With God, there is always more!) It is to us, the church, that she also refers. And it is to you, a baptized Christian, another Christ, that she says, "The body of Christ." And it is to this action of sharing, of feeding and being food, to which she refers: The body of Christ.

To accept such a great mystery — that this bread, as ordinary as it is, has become Christ's body; that we, as fractured a church as we are, have become Christ's body; that I, as unworthy as I am, have become Christ's body; that this simple, human gesture of sharing a morsel of bread builds and sustains Christ's body — to accept such a mystery we say with all our heart, Amen! Let it be done to us, to me, according to your word.

And so that the body may have abundant life and be strong, strong in the face of death, another minister presents to all of us and to each of us the cup. He says our other name: "The blood of Christ." He speaks of this consecrated wine, he speaks of this church, of martyrs ancient and modern, he speaks of you. He speaks of this most intimate sharing, this simple action of sharing from a common cup that so profoundly seals our destiny and changes us forever.

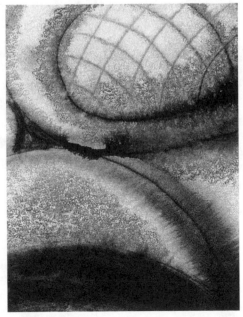

I may not know you, may not know your other names or the details of your struggles. But bound to you by baptism, I take up the cup from which you have drunk, and I, too, drink, and another one drinks after me and another one after that until all have done so. That baptismal bond is being drawn tighter. We are one. Your struggles are mine. Mine are yours. And all is Christ's—including the victory.

And we are changed—and are changing. We become Christ's body, bread broken for a world that is obese with materialism and still dying of malnutrition. We become a leaven in the world's bread, an agent of change that helps the reign of God to rise, fragrantly, like a loaf browning in the oven. We become Christ's blood, wine poured out in sacrifice and in celebration, poured out for the sake of a world drowning in division and still dying of thirst, a thirst for union and *communion.* We become the brewer's yeast, the zest that unlocks the extraordinary in the ordinary, the tingle that makes sober people giddy with joy, the sweet smell and taste of the vintage.

Such transformation, such transubstantiation—of the bread, of the wine, of you, of me, of the church, of *us*—such change is possible because Christ says so: "This—*and you*—my body. This—*and you*—the cup of my blood. Do this and remember me."

Do this! Made bold by this command, let us go to the table that is Christ. Let us go and fervently pray there, "Send your Spirit upon these gifts to make them holy, that they may become"— *and by sharing them that we may be*—"the body and blood of our Lord Jesus Christ, at whose command we celebrate this eucharist." Then will the Spirit whisper through the church, calling each of us and all of us by those names so dear to God: The body of Christ. The blood of Christ. Then we will answer as Bishop Augustine taught us to, by saying Amen to what we are.

The body of Christ.

The blood of Christ.

Amen.

Amen.

Amen.

KEEPING SILENCE

There are different kinds of quiet. Have you ever noticed how the silence of the hour before dawn is different than that of midnight? And think of the silences between human beings. Two people can be silent together, and depending on the circumstance, the silence will be different: It will be the angry silence that follows a fight, or the nervous silence that discomforts strangers. It may be the well-worn silence of familiarity or the awkward silence of lovers who can say nothing in the face of the mystery of loving each other. It may be a bored silence, or a thoughtful one; apathy or contemplation.

Silence can be passive: I have nothing to say, so I say nothing. Silence also can be active: I am being quiet on purpose, to focus entirely on you. There is no listening without silence, and no dialogue. There is no gazing without silence, no attentiveness. There is no wonder or awe without a deep silence.

With God, there are different kinds of silence, too. There was that potent silence before God said, "Let there be. . . ." There was the guilty silence of Adam and Eve when God asked, "Where were you when I called to you?" There was the utter silence of the Sabbath when Jesus rested in the tomb.

We are silent sometimes before God, ashamed of what we have or haven't done. We often are silent before God, overtaken by wonder. We try to be silent before God in order to hear the word and ponder it in our hearts. Alone and together, we practice silence before God: a silence that begets dialogue, a silence that leads us to listen, a silence that soars like awe and like love.

In the liturgy, we are silent, silent *together.* This is not an individual silence, even though each of us—as best as each of us is able—is quiet. This is not a passive silence, even though we try to be as still as we can be. We are silent together, actively quiet, purposely still. We're silent before the liturgy begins, in order to be present to each other and thus find God. God is always present to us; we forget this sometimes and fail to hear

God amid our noisy living. So before we wrestle with God in our rites, we are silent: Be still, and know that I am God.

We are silent at the words "Let us pray." These words begin the opening prayer and the prayer after communion at Mass, as well as the prayers after the psalms at Morning and Evening Prayer. At this invitation, we pray, and we pray hard, and we do so together, so that when the priest speaks, all of our prayers are drawn to those words like metal shavings to a magnet. One voice breaks the silence with words of prayer, and one mighty voice, spoken from all our throats, seals that prayer: "Amen!"

We are silent after readings of scripture and after the homily. How else can God speak to us? How else are we to hear the divine voice, not only echoing from long ago in ancient words brought back to life, but speaking now, in this time, in the quiet that we provide here? After the readings and the homily, we are silent together because we are listening together for the voice on which our very lives depend, the voice that calls us into being, the voice that bids us to come out of our dumb tombs to live and to love again.

On occasion, instead of singing, we may be silent when the gifts of money are gathered for the poor and for the church, and when the gifts of bread and wine are brought to the altar. And when all have been fed, when all have drunk from the cup, again we are silent, caught up in the revery of great mystery, standing together wide-eyed and satisfied, breathing quiet gratitude for life breaking out everywhere, enjoying the quiet of this moment before an eternal dawn, when God will be all in all and the final silence will be ruptured with raucous, joyous cries of "Worthy! Worthy! Worthy!"

The liturgy's silences both tax and nourish us. They tire us because they are active moments, concentrated periods of deliberate, attentive, awe-filled stillness. But they nourish us as well. The moments of communal silence in the liturgy plant seeds of peace in our souls, so that in the turmoil of everyday life, we can find a still center inside and hear the voice of God.

So we are going to practice being silent, being silent together. We are going to recollect ourselves after greeting each other and taking our seats. We are going to pause at the invitation, "Let us pray." We are going to wait on God's word—everybody from usher to choir member, sitting down, sitting still, for a healthy period of silence after each reading from scripture and then after the homily. And again, after the paschal meal, we will share a communion of quiet, a silence as joyful as our singing during communion was exuberant.

At first, our silence will seem awkward. Throats will cough, seats will creak, song sheets will rattle. But if we stick to it, if we resist the temptation to rush along, eventually our silence will deepen and lengthen. We will come to appreciate the chance to contemplate together, and the liturgy will become less a torrent of words and more a sacred celebration, an encounter with God that has a rhythm of song and speech and silence, of action and rest.

To do this and to do this well, we need to practice being silent at home, alone and with those with whom we live. We need to practice turning off the television, the radio and the stereo. We need to pause for a moment of silence before beginning our prayers. We need to stop and think for a moment in the heat of an argument or a debate. We need to greet the words of others with the attentive silence of the good listener before we respond. And sometimes we need to gaze into each other's eyes, saying nothing, appreciating everything.

If we do these things, if we practice being silent, being silent together, being silent with God, then when death comes, we may be less afraid. We may fear a little less the terrible silence of the end, perhaps even be able to tentatively welcome it. For we will know that death's silence is but the momentary hush before the grand singing of the angels and saints in the new Jerusalem, in whose choir of praise we will find our true voice. And then God will listen, silently as a pleased lover for whom no words will do.

LET US PRAY TO THE LORD

Have you ever pleaded a case on someone else's behalf? Even if you're not a lawyer, at one time or another you've probably stood up for someone else. Maybe you insisted that a health-care bureaucracy take more notice of an elderly or ill friend whose care was being neglected. Or maybe you wrote a letter to the government in support of legislation on behalf of the homeless. Maybe you spoke up for a co-worker unjustly accused of wrongdoing. Or you pestered your friends and co-workers to buy raffle tickets to help the needy. And who hasn't asked for something on behalf of a child who was too shy to ask?

To ask on behalf of someone else, to plead or to beg for the well being of other people — especially people who, for whatever reason, are unable to ask or plead or beg for themselves — is a noble act. When we do so in prayer, it's called "making intercession," and intercessory prayer is an important Christian responsibility. In fact, intercessory prayer is so important that it has a prominent role in the Mass and the Liturgy of the Hours, the church's daily prayer.

An important part of Mass and daily prayer is the "general intercessions," often called "the prayers of the faithful." In daily prayer, the general intercessions follow the psalms and gospel canticle. In addition to the prayers of the faithful that follow the homily at Mass, there also are intercessions woven into the great eucharistic prayer itself. So what are we doing when we offer up prayers for the church and for the world, for those oppressed by their needs, and for the city, parish and neighborhood?

The scripture readings in the liturgy proclaim and present the reign of God. So at Mass we hear that, with the coming of God, the blind will be able to watch the lame dance, the mute will sing and the deaf will hear the song, children will be safe from all harm, no one will be without life's necessities and joys,

the earth will be tended with care, and creation itself will live in harmony. Then we stand before God and admit in concrete terms that this is not happening everywhere and for everyone — a consequence not of God's will but of human choices and of sin, both social and individual.

We begin to see the world with Christ's eyes and hear it with Christ's ears. We cannot ignore the pain that we see and the anguish that we hear; we may even begin to feel it in our hearts. So we speak up. We speak up for those whose pain is so great, whose struggle is so all-consuming that they might not even be able to speak up for themselves.

And something happens when we speak up. When we make intercession, we begin to stand up for, and more importantly to stand with, the people for whom we intercede. We begin to identify with them, claim them as our sisters and brothers. We plead their case before God, not because God does not know it, and certainly not because God is playing some kind of game with their suffering. That kind of god would not be worth praying to. It's more like this: When a tragedy besets a mutual acquaintance, our impulse is to go to others who know this person and say, "Did you hear. . . ." The others may already know, but we nonetheless recount the details of the tragedy, adding bits and pieces of information to try to make sense of the tragedy. In so doing, even if no new information is gained, a concern greater than our own individual sympathy is generated and magnified. Perhaps some form of action is agreed to: Together, we'll do this for our friend in need.

That's what happens in intercessory prayer. God knows what we need before we even say it. But by saying it, we begin to act like Christ, who suffered with those who suffered and who lifted up the poor and needy as he himself was lifted up on the

cross, begging forgiveness for the whole world, even his execu-
tioners, and pleading the case for all sinners, including us. When
we make intercession for others, empathy and compassion are
generated and magnified.

At daily prayer, the intercessions follow the singing of the
psalms and the gospel canticle. Have you ever noticed that
sometimes at daily prayer we sing a psalm that does not match
our own circumstances? We sing the psalm of an old person
waiting to die, even though we may be young and healthy. Or
we sing the psalm of a person beset by unjust enemies, even
though we may live at peace. Or in another psalm we sing the
words of a person who feels utterly abandoned by God and by
friends, even though life is good for us right now. The psalms
teach us how to intercede for others, because they show us how
to sing the pain and joys of others as well as our own, to join our
voices to the voices of the poor and the oppressed, to the voices
of the happy and the holy.

So, following the psalms and the gospel canticle —
Zechariah's Benedictus in the morning and Mary's Magnificat in
the evening — we make intercession. We give voice to the
voiceless cries of the suffering and the poor. We stand in their
place, even if but momentarily; we stand up for them and we
stand together with them. And we stand ready, ready to become
part of God's answer to our prayers.

For we cannot ask God to feed the hungry if we are not
willing to share from our own tables. And we dare not ask God
to shelter the homeless without being willing to open our own
doors. And we would be hypocrites to ask God to heal the sick
without wanting to be God's instruments of healing and care. So
it is serious business, making intercession. It's about experiencing the world as Christ experiences it, and it's about loving the
world as Christ loves it — utterly and selflessly.

This is how it works. The deacon — whose ministry outside of the liturgy is especially geared toward those in need — or
the cantor or the lector announces the general petition: "For all
those who are unemployed . . ." or "For the sick. . . ." Our job
is to focus our minds and hearts at that moment to include in that
general intercession all those that we know or that we have

heard about, to hold them up to God in this prayer. And not just family members and friends, either. We must strive to include people that we don't know but about whom we've heard from others, from the radio or television. Our intercessions must reach far and wide, so our compassion and love will, too.

That's why it could be argued that Christians have an obligation to scan the newspaper or catch the evening news as a prerequisite to praying together. Mindful that these media also influence our perception of events and our reactions to the people involved, we must nonetheless be aware of other people's joys and pains, successes and failures, triumphs and tragedies. Careful to avoid letting the media decide who is our friend and who is our enemy, who is deserving of our concern and who is not (remember Jesus' answer to the question, "Who is my neighbor?"), we must bring the needs and concerns, the hopes and the yearnings of the world to God in prayer.

Even Christians who enter the cloister to devote themselves to contemplation still make intercessory prayer on behalf of the needy. And Christians who are ill or homebound because of advanced age still share the responsibility of offering up their own suffering on behalf of others who suffer. The intercessory prayers of the sick are particularly powerful: The love that they express selflessly transcends their own suffering to reach out and embrace others who are also in need. That kind of self-sacrifice is Christ's indeed.

"Bear one another's burdens," Saint Paul reminds us. Indeed the heart of the paschal mystery is that God has freely chosen to bear with us the human burden of suffering and death, and in so doing has redeemed those experiences, turning evil into good, death into life. We begin to bear one another's burdens here, in this place, in this hour, when the deacon or cantor bids us, "Let us pray to the Lord," and with one voice we reply, "Lord, hear our prayer."

WE BRING YOU THESE GIFTS

Despite the fact that shopping for Christmas gifts can be stressful, and that choosing the right gift for a neighbor whom we may not know well enough causes a bit of anxiety, we like giving gifts. We know that making or purchasing and wrapping a gift is a physical manifestation of a spiritual reality: an appreciation of the person to whom it is given, a celebration of this person and what she or he means to us, a symbol — the gift and the giving — that not only expresses the love that we have for the person but that actually deepens that love, widens it, strengthens it, inspires it, invigorates it.

I give you a gift because I have come to know that you are a gift, a gift to me, a gift to the world; that no one ever or anywhere else is you, that no one gives me what you give me, means to me what you mean to me.

And thus, despite the anxiety that making or purchasing gifts for each other causes, we nonetheless enter into gift-giving with at least a modicum of enthusiasm, a bit of excitement, an ounce of hope that the love that we share is indeed what is ultimate.

And so it is in the assembly of the church. And so it is when we — as individuals, yes, and more so, as a people — give our gifts to God. But what do you give to a god? What do you give to the Living God who made everything and has everything and needs nothing?

We offer the simple things of bread and wine, "which earth has given and human hands have made." We used to call the point in the Mass when the bread and the wine are brought forward "the offertory." But now we call it the preparation, because that's in fact what happens then: We prepare the Lord's table and we prepare our gift of money for the poor and for the church, and we prepare our gifts of bread and wine to give to God. The offering of these gifts happens later, in the great eucharistic prayer.

So what is being offered under the sign of bread and wine? What is the gift behind the gift? We take our clue from what the priest says to begin the great prayer of thanksgiving: "Lift up your hearts." That is what is invested in our bread and in our wine — our hearts, that lovely ancient metaphor for "all of me," for "all of us." That, in fact, is the gift that we bring. That is what we offer — our hearts, our very selves under the sign of bread and wine. And that is what God accepts. That is what the mighty Creator, the awesome Shekinah, the ultimate Mystery and holy Wisdom accepts from us. And that is what the God of Jesus changes into Christ's body and blood to give back to us.

The offering in the great eucharistic prayer becomes an exchange. We give to God our hearts, under the sign of bread and wine. In return God gives back to us the body and blood of Christ, under the same sign. And so we have the old, lovely image in the eucharistic prayer called "the Roman canon": "We pray that your angel may take this sacrifice to your altar in heaven. Then as we receive from this altar the sacred body and blood of your son, let us be filled with every grace and blessing."

We must not be stingy when we enter into this divine exchange of gifts. We must prepare to give God the full gift: our whole heart, as individuals and as a church. We must see in this bread our successes and our struggles, and see in this wine our passion and our pain. These experiences are given to God and changed and given back to us. And we are changed in the giving and in the receiving, changed for the sake of the world, changed for the sake of the reign of God that is now and not-yet, here and still-to-come. We become a living sacrifice of praise, bread for the world, wine for the weary.

So when you come into church, stop by the gifts table. Extend your hands over that bread. Place onto that bread your accomplishments of this week, the job that you did well (the wall that you painted, the meal that you prepared), the simple acts of kindness that you performed, the work in which this parish engages (food delivered to the needy, children taught to read).

Then this is consecrated with the bread, returned to you as your life made holy, to us as our life made holy, so that this parish, this city, this world may be made holy: the mystical body of Christ.

Extend your hands over that wine. Place in that flagon your struggles: the addiction you resisted, the harm you healed. Place in that flagon this parish's struggles: halting steps toward being a more inclusive community, small attempts to be more faithful to the gospel. Then this is consecrated with the wine, returned to us a cup of salvation: this blood poured out once and for all so that the blood of our children may never again stain our streets, so that the blood of the convict need not be shed in revenge, so that the blood of soldiers need never be wasted in far-away fields.

And when we are invited to lift up our hearts, let us — each of us and all of us — do so consciously, remembering what we have invested in these gifts, what it is in fact that we are bringing to God. And let us pray without hesitation, with sincerity and with great devotion, "And so Father, we bring you these gifts. We ask you to bless them and to make them holy."

CALLING TO MIND AND READY TO GREET HIM

Part of what it means to be human is that we remember things. Sure, the swallows remember to return to San Juan Capistrano in California each spring, and the monarch butterflies remember to make their way to Mexico for the winter. However, such remembering in animals and insects is more the gracious gift of a provident Creator than an act on the part of the creature. God has inscribed such memories in instincts for survival. But we humans remember different things in different ways, and some things we remember deliberately.

I remember what I ate for dinner last night—rice and beans, or pierogi and kielbasa, or meatloaf and mashed potatoes. That's simply a fact that I call up from a file in my brain. I don't necessarily have any emotional attachment to this fact, nor do I have any enduring sense experience—unless the food was so spicy that I was up all night!

I also remember the first time that I realized I loved someone. This kind of remembering involves the calling up of facts and details—it was in this place, on this day of that year. But it also involves something more. The very act of calling to mind this episode brings with it a renewed sense of that initial experience, that queasy, uneasy feeling. And I may even have a physical reaction now, similar or identical to the one I had then—goosebumps! If the love is still alive, calling to mind its origin makes that origin present. Despite the years that have passed, the first moment that I realized this love is a reality that lives on outside of time. We remember some things collectively, too: On the fourth of July in the United States we remember the Continental Congress' stand for independence. So we participate in a parade or a picnic. And although that event—the signing of the Declaration of Independence—is in the past, it affects the present by making it possible: The past event has created a community of people with a common history who celebrate something of their origins on this day, in this year and in coming years. It's more than mere historical commemoration. And it's certainly not historical reenactment. In fact, we may not even think about the drafting and debating, the amending, voting and signing. But the fruits of all that — community, identity, leisure, celebration (with fireworks!) — are not some abstract and irrelevant historical footnote. They are a living legacy that the past gives to the present, to shape us, renewing the common bond as well as refreshing individuals. And the celebration then orients us toward the future: We go back to our routine on the fifth of July a bit more relaxed, a bit more grateful, eager for the next holiday, but ready, if not willing, to work until then!

We draw on all of these different ways of remembering to remember Jesus. We learn his story. We call to mind how we first came to experience Jesus in prayer, in doing good works, in the events of our lives. And most importantly, we remember Jesus together, on Sunday, in the assembly of the church, in the liturgy. And, in this calling to mind, something wondrous happens. When we together call on the Holy Spirit to remember Jesus, Jesus is present. The events of the past live in the present. And they show us the future.

This great act of remembering happens at Mass in the heart of the liturgy, the eucharistic prayer. Speaking to God, we recall all that Jesus did, and so we give thanks and praise. It's a very human way of acting. When I give you a gift that you especially love, you rave about it. You go on and on about how perfect it is, even enumerating its qualities. Of course, I know these things — I'm the one who gave it to you. But somehow we both take delight in you making such a fuss. You are thrilled with the gift, and I am thrilled that you are thrilled. A spirit moves among us, generating an electricity that binds us closer to each other and that invests the gift with a value beyond its monetary worth.

So it is in church: When we are gathered, when we have listened to the scriptures, when we have collected gifts for the poor and for the church, when we have set forth bread and wine, we call on the Holy Spirit.

The Spirit helps us call to mind all that God has done for us: creating a cosmos, planting a garden, calling a people, ransoming slaves, speaking through prophets, anointing leaders, suffering with the poor and the dejected. The Spirit helps us call to mind all that God has done for us in Jesus, especially his last supper, his passion on the cross, his dying to save us and his rising from the dead. By the power of the Holy Spirit, when we call to mind these saving deeds done once for all, the past lives in the present. We are not reenacting Christ's passion, death and resurrection, like some historical pageant. We are experiencing it here, in this place and time, under these signs: a church gathered to remember, sacred stories told, bread and wine offered, body and blood received.

Such active remembering we call *anamnesis,* a Greek word that means "making memorial." Anamnesis is a part of every eucharistic prayer. In fact, it is an important element of all prayer in both the Jewish and Christian traditions. We have a *living* memory of what God has done for us. And through this living memory, God comes to us — here, today. We are at no disadvantage because we live 2000 years after Jesus walked on earth. Our living memory — itself a gift from God — saves us:

> Father, we now celebrate this *memorial*
> of our redemption. We *recall* Christ's death,
> his descent among the dead, his resurrection,
> and his ascension to your right hand;
> *and, looking forward* to his coming in glory,
> *we offer* you his body and blood,
> the acceptable sacrifice
> which brings salvation to the whole world.

Notice that this eucharistic prayer says that we recall *and* look forward as we *now* make this offering. Another eucharistic prayer says it this way:

> Father, *calling to mind* the death your Son
> endured for our salvation,
> his glorious resurrection and ascension into heaven,
> *and ready to greet him* when he comes again,
> *we offer you* in thanksgiving this holy and living
>   sacrifice.

So our remembering is not a dead nostalgia: "Remember good old Jesus and the good old days? He sure was something, wasn't he?" Our remembering is a *living* memory, an encounter with Jesus here and now. When we call to mind Christ's saving deeds, those deeds of long ago become the very deeds that we do here and now: Christ gathered a community; we assemble as a parish. Christ preached the good news; we proclaim and ponder the scriptures. Christ was lifted up nailed to the cross; we lift up a loaf of bread and a cup of wine. Christ died; we break the loaf of bread and pour out the flagon of wine. Christ rose from the dead; we share the bread of life and the saving cup. The risen Christ breathed the Spirit on the apostles; we are made bold by the banquet that we share, bold to tell Christ's story by the way we live our lives, by the way we love those that the world deems unworthy of being loved.

The saving deeds of the past become the deeds we do in the present: Christ *has* died; Christ *is* risen. And we do these deeds today in order to bring about a better tomorrow: Christ *will* come again. Our living memory helps us give birth to the future. Our living memory builds up the reign of God where no one — no matter how small or poor — is forgotten, where no love will ever fade from memory or fail to satisfy.

When the priest summons us in the eucharistic prayer, let us gather and exercise our living memory of Jesus. Let us call to mind Christ's great saving deeds of long ago. But let us also remember how Christ has acted out those deeds in our own lives this past week. How and from whom have you heard the good news this week: the word that affirmed you when you felt worthless, the word that challenged you when you felt like you had everything under control? How were you lifted up and nailed to the cross this past week? How did you die to your self in order to live for another? Think of these things that happened to you this week.

Then we will be true to the words that we pray. Then we will be ready to greet Christ when he comes again in this hour, in this eucharist, and when he comes again in the final hour, the hour of our death, the hour of the end. Then our living memory will become eternal living.

LET YOUR SPIRIT COME UPON THESE GIFTS

How do you know that the wind exists? You hear a howling down the street or a whispering through the branches of trees. You see the window shake. You feel the rush of air. You smell things far away, taste dust in your mouth or wipe the tears from your eyes. But you never hear, see, touch, smell or taste *wind.*

How do we know that the Holy Spirit exists? We hear enemies who were dead set against each other apologize. We see someone who was dead in an addiction rise to make it through

the day sober. We touch the shoulder of a friend and know that we'll face his terminal illness together. We smell the sweetness of spring blossoming out of winter's death. We sip wine, eat a bit of freshly baked bread and are revived. And thus we hear, see, feel, smell and taste the Holy Spirit.

So, too, in our rites we come to hear and see, touch, smell and taste the Holy Spirit. And the Holy Spirit sounds a lot like a hymn sung with gusto, a chant floating in the air. The Holy Spirit looks like the newly baptized, dripping wet and shivering as they emerge from the font. The Holy Spirit feels like the hug or hand-shake we exchange in peace. The Holy Spirit smells like the balsamic perfume of chrism oil dripping from the heads of the anointed. And the Holy Spirit tastes like this bread, this wine of the eucharist.

Notice what we pray in the great eucharistic prayer. After we lift up our hearts; after we give God thanks and praise; after we acclaim God and God alone as holy, holy, holy; after we call to mind Jesus, then the priest extends both hands, palms down-ward, over the loaf of our bread, over the cup and flagon of our wine and says, "Let your Spirit come upon these gifts to make them holy, so that they may become for us the body and blood of our Lord, Jesus Christ."

Do we have any sense of what it is we do when we do this? "Let your Spirit come upon these gifts." What sort of power are we invoking here, with words that seem so plain and a ges-ture—the laying on of hands, as scripture calls it—a gesture so seemingly simple?

On our bread, on our wine, we are calling down the same Spirit that brooded over the swirling chaos before God's voice said, "Let there be. . . ." On our bread, on our wine we are call-ing down the same Spirit that breathed into the mud pies that God had fashioned on the river bank, causing them to spring to life, to dance and to sing. On our bread, on our wine we are calling down the same Spirit that inhabited Huldah and jumped Jeremiah, the same Spirit that struck Zechariah dumb and made Mary sing. On our bread, on our wine we are calling down the same Spirit that overshadowed Mary, swelling her womb with life until she gave birth to God in the flesh. On our bread, on our wine we are calling down the same Spirit that seeped from Jesus' nostrils when he died on the cross, and that poured from his lips when he said "Peace" to frightened disciples three days later. On our bread, on our wine, we are calling down the same Spirit that shook the house and inflamed the hearts of the apostles on the day of Pentecost. It's that Spirit, that power, that we call down upon this bread, this wine.

Not only do we call the Holy Spirit down upon our bread and wine to change them (although that would be wondrous enough), we also call the Holy Spirit down upon *us,* so that we, too, may be changed: "Grant that we, who are nourished by his body and blood, may be filled with his Holy Spirit, and become one body, one spirit in Christ." If we are amazed at the thought of the Holy Spirit coming down upon our bread, upon our wine, we should be absolutely awestruck at the notion that this same Spirit, this powerful Spirit, is called down upon us! Think of what will happen when we focus on these words that we say, when we say them with our hearts as well as our lips, mean them with our minds as well as our mouths! What will happen to us when God takes us at our word and answers our prayer? When the Holy Spirit comes down upon us as we eat and drink this Spirit food?

Nothing less than this: Enemies will be reconciled, prisoners rehabilitated, the condemned pardoned, addicts freed, the sick cured, the ignorant instructed, the hungry fed, the naked clothed, the homeless sheltered, the immigrants welcomed. Women will be treated with full human dignity, and children will be spared abuse. Self-righteousness and selfishness will dry up and blow away. Concern for the common good will become the real political motivation. And dead people — *dead people* — will dance and sing.

Here we go. In a few moments we will pray these words: Send your Spirit upon these gifts to make them holy, to make us holy, so that they, yes, but also that by sharing them *we* may become the body and blood, one body, one spirit in Christ. Are we ready? Here we go.

THROUGH HUMAN HANDS

Human hands talk. Even when our mouths are silent and our lips sealed, our hands tell everybody who can see them how we are feeling. They're clenched into fists, showing anger. Or they're clammy, with fidgeting fingers, tattling about how nervous we are. They touch another person softly, whispering love. They sting another with a slap, spitting venom. Some say that without hands, Italians wouldn't be able to talk at all. But that's true of all of us. And those among us who are without hearing literally talk with their hands.

And in so speaking, our hands manufacture meaning: A fist doesn't merely *show* that I'm angry; clenching my hands into fists *makes* me angry. A gentle caress does more than just *show* that I love you; it actually *makes* me love you *more.* Our spirits are not disembodied; body and soul are one. What happens with our hands happens in our hearts and heads as well. Our thinking and our feeling are shaped by the holding and the letting go that we do with our hands. We know the world by touching it. We are all blind in various degrees, and we search for meaning with our hands. Like fingertips reading braille letters, we rub our temples in fatigue, we pat each other on the back to congratulate or reassure, we clasp hands to bid welcome or farewell, we touch to diagnose and to heal. Community is created when we join hands, when the advantaged give the disadvantaged a hand up, when all hands work together for the common good. Human hands create community.

Maybe this is why the Holy Spirit chooses to communicate through human hands. The laying on of hands is the sacred sign by which the Holy Spirit now moves among us.

This is wonderful. Think of it! In the beginning, in that time before time, the Holy Spirit *brooded* over the waters — perched on this planet like a hen warming her eggs — and life itself was born. And later, that same Spirit *overshadowed* the young virgin: Salvation ripened in her womb and life everlasting was born. Like a dove, the Spirit *hovered* over Jesus, baptized by John in the Jordan. Like a last gasp, the Spirit *descended* from Jesus' lips onto the church at the foot of the cross: "Into your hands, I commend my spirit." Like wind and fire, the Spirit *howled* and *licked* at the church huddled in the upper room. Then eternity was put within our reach; the task of building a new earth was put squarely into our hands — these hands, our hands, the hands of the body of Christ. The powerful Spirit of God, the invisible Spirit of God, the uncontrollable Spirit of God communicates with the world now by the touch of human hands: The risen Christ imparts the Holy Spirit through the laying on of hands.

The Spirit freely moves when we lay hands, when we fall silent before God, open up our hearts, focus our prayer, direct our attention and extend our hands over something, or place our hands on someone's head. And where the Spirit moves, things happen: Things — and people — change, life throbs and pulses and overflows. We extend our hands over the water in our font, and the Spirit changes the flood of chaos into the river of life, the deadly whirlpool into the bath of baptism. We lay hands on those we have baptized, and the Spirit changes each Adam, each Eve into Christ. We lay hands on the head of one who repents, and the Spirit forgives sin and restores the sinner to communion. We lay hands on the sick, anointing them with oil, and the Spirit heals and consoles and restores. We lay hands on the heads of those we ordain, and the Spirit creates deacons, priests and bishops to nourish order and service in the church. And we extend our hands over our gifts of bread and wine — we lay hands on them — and by the Spirit bread and wine become for us the body and blood of Christ. In so doing, we also extend our hands over the assembled church, and the Spirit gathers into one body all who believe.

The same Spirit that brooded and overshadowed, hovered and descended and howled now moves — peacefully but no less powerfully — through the laying on of hands, these hands, our hands, the hands of the body of Christ. As it is in the assembly of the church, so it will be out in the world when we leave here:

The Spirit will move through our hands to build up and to bless, to create and to console and to consecrate. So the hammer and the knitting needle, the spatula and the telephone that you pick up become tools for building a new earth, the new Jerusalem. And each time you pat a shoulder, rub a head of hair or clasp another hand in greeting, you send out sparks and feel the shock of the Spirit. Perhaps all that Midas touched turned to gold, but all that we touch can turn to good, if we open ourselves up to the power of God coursing through us in the laying on of hands.

It is not automatic or magical, though. We must open ourselves to the Spirit and cooperate if our touch is to impart life and not deal death, if our touch is to heal and not harm. Too often today, wives are touched violently by their husbands, and children are touched inappropriately by trusted adults. Too often the elderly and the sick are handled roughly, without dignity. Too often today when we touch the surfaces of our city — the seat on the train, the sidewalk, the park bench — we scar them with graffiti, litter them with food wrappers, or break and pick at them. Too often today when we touch creation, we poison and pollute instead of tending with care.

In itself, human touch is very ambiguous. But by God's Spirit, human touch is redeemed. By the power of the Spirit, human touch is transformed and made a vehicle for the touch of God. The ritual gesture of the laying on of hands can communicate healing to a world slapped by hate. The laying on of hands can help us know that the God who lives beyond our grasp is also the God who is at hand, in these hands, our hands. All of our deeds, all of our doings, all of our actions and activities find their deepest purposes in the laying on of hands. For in our hands, God places life and love and the future. May we handle them with care.

THE LIFTING UP OF MY HANDS

Prayer is the heart's business, it is true. And the head's, too. But it also is an activity of the body. When Jacob spent the night praying at Peniel, his prayers literally turned into a wrestling match with an angel. As the day began to break, the angel wanted to depart, but Jacob would not quit. Jacob knew that to pray was to reach for God and to wrestle with God and to not let go — until receiving a blessing. Prayer is something that we do, as much as it is something that we think and feel. In fact, the thinking and feeling of prayer may not even be possible if we don't first *do* something — in and with our bodies. That is why at various liturgies we walk in procession, we stand and we sit, we bow and we kneel: What we do with our bodies nurtures what is in our minds and hearts and souls. How can we live our lives as pilgrims in this world if we never walk a pilgrimage? And how do we know that we adore God if we never bow our heads or bend our knees before the divine?

From our Semitic ancestors we have inherited a tradition, a way of praying with our hands as well as our hearts. From the Latin word for "praying," this posture is called *orans:* You stand up straight, raise your eyes and lift up your arms, hands open, palms up. The first Christians used this posture regularly and found it full of meaning. In fact, the third-century theologian Origen wrote:

> Even more than stretching out the hands, one must lift up the soul heavenward. More than raising up the eyes, one must lift up the spirit to God. For there can be no doubt that among a thousand possible positions of the body, outstretched hands and uplifted eyes are to be preferred above all others, so imaging forth in the body those directions of the soul.

At the same time, the theologian Tertullian taught that to stand and pray in this way was to be an image of the crucified Christ: "Not only do we raise our hands," he wrote, "but we raise them in a cross like our Lord in his passion, and by this attitude we confess Christ."

Over the centuries this form of body prayer survived as a gesture made only by the priest when he prayed on behalf of the church. Even today, you see the priest pray the collect prayers and the great eucharistic prayer in this way. In medieval times, lay people adopted a new posture, the custom of Frankish servants who knelt down in front of their lords and folded their hands together in front of their breasts. This was an innovation.

But there is no rule, no reason, why we cannot, do not all pray in the orans position. Origen and Tertullian were correct: This body prayer is full of meaning. We stand humbly before God. Our eyes look to heaven. Our hands are empty and our arms are open, ready to receive what God gives us, ready to embrace God, who comes to us — sometimes like an angel with whom we must wrestle but most often in another human being, longing to be embraced.

Standing this way, lifting up our hands, we stand like Christ. We stand like Christ who stood with arms outstretched to hug children and gather the lepers fearlessly to his heart. We stand like Christ who stretched out his arms in a cosmic embrace, suspended on the tree between heaven and earth, loving us to the death, drawing all things to himself. And we stand like Christ rising beyond death to eternal life, drawing all things to God. What power such a stance has! To stand *like* Christ before God is to stand *with* Christ before God, and we know that with Christ, through Christ and in Christ, God hears our prayers.

So let us all stand this way when the great eucharistic prayer is prayed. Thus we are ready to serve God at this table and in the world. Thus are we willing to offer up our very bodies along with our bread and wine, and in turn, receive from God the body and the blood. And let us all stand this way when we pray the words that Christ taught us. Let us stand as Christ

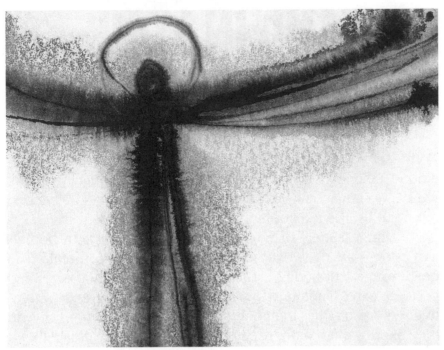

stood and pray as Christ prayed, calling on God, our Father—here in the assembly of the church, and at home. For in so doing, little by little, we are made like Christ.

Augustine teaches us:

> Lift up your hands in prayer! Our Lord lifted up his hands on the cross for us and extended his hands for us. His hands were opened on the cross so that our hands might be opened in good works. . . . The apostle says, "Lift up clean hands, without wrath and deception." So when you lift your hands to God, they should remind you of your works.

Lifting up our hands, Sunday after Sunday, we open ourselves to the Spirit who propels us from this table back into the streets. And there, with our eyes fixed always on heaven, we will open our hands to hold abandoned babies and our arms to cuddle abused children. And we will gather close to ourselves those suffering from AIDS and from Alzheimer's disease. Lifting up our hands to heaven each day at home, we lift up all those whom we have touched, and from our arms God will take the sorrowing and the suffering, and redeem them.

TO STAND IN YOUR PRESENCE

"Why are you Catholics always up and down at your service?" a non-Catholic friend asked after a Catholic wedding. We stand, we sit, we bow, we kneel, we walk in procession—it's second nature to us. But the question of why is a good one.

Liturgy is more than words: It is an action done by bodies, as a body—the body of Christ. It is corporeal and corporate. The postures that our bodies assume *mean* something. Postures and gestures express intangible realities: respect, reverence, attentiveness (or apathy, indifference, boredom). And not only do they express these inner experiences, they actually create them. Yawning doesn't just express my boredom, it makes me bored!

Standing is a posture so utilitarian that it almost seems silly to speak of it. But what a human accomplishment it was when our ancestors stiffened their necks and straightened their backs to greet a new era, to take a new place—literally head and shoulders above the rest of creation—as creatures made in the image and likeness of God. Think of all the things that you couldn't do if you couldn't stand up!

Our daily language reveals some of the significance that standing has come to have for us. We stand up for what we believe. We stand against evil and injustice. We stand in for others who cannot fulfill a responsibility. We stand by those whom we trust. We stand with those with whom we agree or whom we support or pity or love. And there are some things for which we simply cannot stand. United we stand, divided we fall.

Standing in contemporary Western culture—as in many other cultures—is a sign of respect. We stand when someone important enters the room. We stand when introduced to someone new. We stand to greet a loved one. We stand when the national anthem is sung.

If you ever doubt that standing expresses and creates respect, try this: Next time you are at a sporting event, stay seated during the singing of the national anthem. If you're not baptized with Budweiser, someone will surely remark about your *disre*spect. Or try this: Next time you are in court, kneel when the judge enters the room. Then explain to the judge that standing is irreverent as you are jailed for contempt of court!

We also stand to be attentive. "Ten-hut," the soldier shouts, and all snap upright to acknowledge the fact that an officer has entered, *and* to prepare to hear and carry out orders. We "stand guard" against dangers, staying awake and alert. We stand still to catch a sound or check something out or think something through.

But standing to be attentive is only a prelude to standing ready to move. Have you ever been seated at your work station when someone comes in and chats incessantly? Stand up; the chatting will come to an end. Why? With your body, you've just said, "It's time to end this and move on." What are you doing when you're "standing around"? Usually, you are waiting for something to happen, for someone to come so that you can go somewhere together.

It's only natural then that we stand when we do at Mass. We stand to begin, to show respect for the gathered assembly. Jesus said, "When two or three are gathered in my name, there I am." As all have gathered for this liturgy, we stand to say, "Christ is here; let Christ's body be joined, and let that body begin this liturgy!" Our respect for Christ's presence in the gathered assembly includes a healthy respect for the presence of Christ in the ordained ministers who lead our assembly.

Next we stand to welcome the gospel. As the deacon lifts the beautiful book, we jump to our feet and sing the song of angels and saints: Alleluia! As the deacon carries the book through this room, we stand, and, if we cannot actually leave our seats to follow it in procession, at least we pivot in place to follow the gospel on its way to the ambo. We stand at attention to hear the good news; we stand ready to live by it and to give our lives for its purposes.

We show respect for God by standing up straight when we ask for things in the prayers of the faithful. In fact, we stand any time that the presider says "Let us pray." And we also stand ready to be part of God's answer to those prayers.

Around the world, most churches stand for the heart of the liturgy — the great eucharistic prayer, in some places kneeling only briefly when Jesus' words at the Last Supper are spoken. (Kneeling at this part of the great prayer is a thirteenth-century innovation — a pretty recent one in a 2000-year-old church!) And some churches in this country have reclaimed the ancient posture, standing throughout the entire prayer. Why do this?

It seems to be the original posture for both clergy and laity during the eucharistic prayer. The first eucharistic prayer — dating back to the early centuries of the church at Rome — asks God to remember "the people for whom we now pray, and all of us standing around *(omnium circumstantium)* [this altar]," who firmly believe in God, dedicate themselves to God and are thus offering themselves as a living sacrifice of praise. The English translation of the second eucharistic prayer, also a very ancient text, says to God, "We thank you for counting us worthy to stand in your presence and serve you."

The posture was not coincidental. We stand in God's presence precisely because we are God's servants. Does a waiter sit (or kneel) at the table that she or he is serving? Standing, besides being a posture of respect, is the stance of service, an active posture that says we are not simply watching this deed, we are participating in it, we are serving its purposes.

Standing in the early church also was understood to be a sign of the risen Christ, so the assembly stood for the eucharistic prayer. In fact, scholars think that not only did the whole assembly stand during the eucharistic prayer, but all stood with outstretched arms, just as the priest continues to do today. This was the bodily way to stand with Christ, by Christ, for Christ.

Standing was considered such an appropriate posture for the eucharistic prayer on Sunday that the Council of Nicaea, meeting in the year 325, forbade kneeling (and fasting) on Sunday. Sunday was not a day to do penance, the Council taught, but a holy day of rejoicing. We stand when giving thanks and praise because Christ was raised from the dead. He was laid low in death, but on Sunday Christ stood victorious over sin and death. We share the paschal meal standing—actually processing—because like the Israelites who were told by God to eat the passover supper with their shoes and coats on and their walking sticks in hand, we, too, are people on a journey, traveling through this life to the promised land of the new Jerusalem, where we will stand together with the angels, the elders, the four creatures and the countless hosts of saints who stand around the throne of the Ancient of Days.

And after we have eaten and drank, after we process back to our places, we *stay* standing until all have shared in the sacrificial supper. Why? This is the moment of communion: one mind, one heart, one voice lifted in song, one posture taken, a unified stance—bodies acting as a body. Notice how at the high points of a game, all the members of the team—even those not playing—stand in excitement to be part of the crucial moment. Notice how people at the climactic conclusion of a well-staged drama stand together offering an ovation. The dynamic here is similar.

We end our liturgy as we began it, standing in the presence of Christ. But now we are ready—like the apostles on Pentecost before us—to spill out of the church's house into the world, embodying the good news, ready to be bread for the hungry and wine for the thirsty.

To stand in the liturgy is to stand as servants of the one who stood up for the poor and the oppressed, the marginalized and the misunderstood. It is to stand with the one who resisted the evil of organized religion colluding with a military government to keep people bent double with heartless customs and oppressive tributes. It is to stand humbly before God who voluntarily bowed down under the wood of the cross so that we might again stand tall, freed from the weight of ancient sin, risen like Christ.

LET US OFFER EACH OTHER A SIGN OF PEACE

When the Second Vatican Council restored the sign of peace as a gesture exchanged among all the faithful, people responded in different ways. Remember the angry worshiper who stood, arms firmly folded, and snarled instead of taking your hand? Remember the extrovert whose goal it was to chit-chat with every single person in church? Remember what happened when the extrovert approached the angry person? For most of us, the sign of peace has become a routine gesture, one that we do without much thought — until someone says that "all that commotion before communion" is disrespectful; or until that Sunday when we are in the awkward position of having to offer a handshake to someone with whom we are angry, or to someone who has hurt us and now happens to be sitting behind us.

Note that the Council *restored* the sign of peace; it is not new. In northern Africa, Augustine knew of the practice in the fourth century. Before that, Paul urged Christians to "greet one another with a holy kiss," although it is not certain that he was speaking about a gesture in the liturgy. He ended some of his letters with that phrase. His letters were read aloud in the assembly, so perhaps he was instructing Christians to share the kiss of peace after the scripture readings.

Many early Christian communities exchanged a kiss of peace at daily prayer, after the prayers of the faithful, or general intercessions. They did so — and some communities still do today — as a pledge: After asking God to care for the needs of the world and the church, the sick and the suffering, the dying and the dead, the kiss of peace is a sign of everyone's and each one's willingness to be part of God's answer to these prayers. So sacred was this kiss of peace in the early ages that people not yet baptized did not offer or receive it. Only after one was baptized did one stay in the room when the kiss of peace was exchanged. Sharing a sign of peace is a duty of baptized persons, because it is Christ's peace — not merely our own — that we share.

In the fifth century, Pope Innocent I taught that the sign of peace was a necessary preparation for those sharing in Christ's body and blood. He also wrote that by sharing the kiss of peace, the people give their consent to all that was prayed in the eucharistic prayer: Like the great Amen, the kiss of peace is a seal of approval.

The kiss of peace never totally disappeared over the centuries. At some Masses before Vatican II the clergy shared a very stylized, graceful embrace. But that gesture of peace — in this country a handshake or a hug, in other countries and cultures a kiss or a bow or an appropriate embrace — is now restored to all of us. And all of us who are baptized have the privilege and the responsibility to offer each other a sign of peace.

So what is it that we are doing when we share the kiss of peace? What does it mean to shake hands with or embrace those around us, to reach out equally to family members, friends and strangers? And what is the significance of any words that we might speak to each other: "Peace be with you." "The peace of Christ." What is this sign of peace?

When we offer each other a sign of *Christ's* peace, we are saying with our bodies that we hold dear the One who is our peace. We are believing with our bodies that the barriers between us have been broken down, the divisions undone, the ruptures repaired. We are pledging with our action that we will leave this place and spread this peace of Christ to the sidewalks and the supermarket aisles, to the dance club and the hospital ward, to the classroom and the laundry room, the barnyard and the library, the laboratory and the dining room, the homeless shelter and the corporate headquarters, the missile factory and the nursery.

There, and in all the places of our lives, we will let this peace diffuse from us like breath from our nostrils, and go forth from us like kind words falling from our lips. For the One who is our peace, the One who rose from the dead—Jesus—breathed on us first, spoke words of peace to us first.

On Easter night, Jesus appeared and breathed on the disciples and said, "Peace is my gift to you." As it has been given to us in baptism and in confirmation, as it is given to us now in this word, as it will be given to us at this table—so do we give it to others. First to each other, here in the assembly of the church, and then to all others—men and women and children, old and young and middle-aged, gay and straight and bisexual, European, African, Asian and American, rich and poor, sick and healthy, educated and ignorant, Christian and Jew and Moslem and Hindu and Buddhist and nonbelievers—and even to creation itself, until that day, that final awesome day, when this kiss of peace shall be all there is.

On that day, creation will be healed into paradise, and each and all of earth's children will be welcomed at the gate, embraced and kissed and ushered to a place at the table in that city of peace, the new Jerusalem.

That dream of peace is born here, in this assembly, in handshakes and hugs offered around this table, in this hour. So when we come to the sign of peace, know who you are and what it is that you do.

Turn to the person next to you, in front of you, behind you. Clasp hands or hug that person as you would embrace Christ himself, for indeed that is what you are doing. And receive from that person the peace of Christ, for that, in fact, is what it is.

And *clasp,* don't *shake* hands. Use both hands, and hold them for a moment, without pumping them. Look into each other's eyes. See in the eyes of this person—this baptized and anointed person—Christ. Exchange a greeting if that feels right: "Peace be with you," or "The peace of Christ."

Don't use this holy moment to chat, or to make plans for breakfast, or even to ask another minister to go get something that has been forgotten. Don't let this holy moment slip by you as though you were a robot going through the motions. Don't share this holy moment only with those whom you know and like. It isn't necessary to greet everyone in the room, either, but do reach broadly. Let's make this holy moment the dawning of

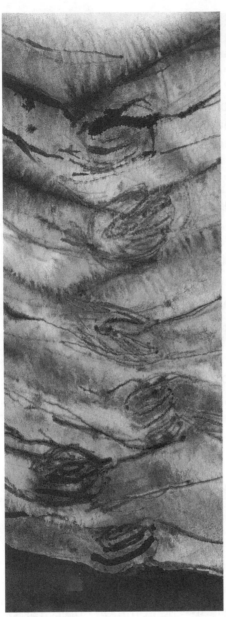

the age of the new Jerusalem, the coming down from heaven of the city of peace. Then will we be ready, then will we be worthy to share in the body and the blood.

Jesus said, "Peace I leave with you, my peace I give to you." Grant us, O God, the peace and unity of the new Jerusalem, where you live forever and ever. Amen.

TAKE AND DRINK

Sometimes we'll take a swig from a beer or soda can of a friend or relative. But our mothers taught us never to let our mouths touch the spigot of the public water fountain, and the common bathroom cup is now long gone. Lovers may share sips of champagne from the same glass. But us? What do you mean that we're all invited to, *supposed* to drink from a common cup in this assembly? Why would Jesus give us such a command: "Take this, all of you, and drink from it. This is the cup of my blood"?

Our sense of unease at drinking from a common cup, from *this* common cup, teaches us something significant but not what we would expect. Different researchers say that "germs" are or are not present in communion cups. And they speculate about the risks of catching a cold, even though no one has ever proven that anything besides communion has been passed on by people drinking from a common chalice. Of course we need to be careful and not cavalier; that's why those of us with colds or communicable illnesses pass by the cup out of respect for others. But it's more than illness that we fear. We hesitate to drink from the cup because we know that this act of taking, drinking and sharing a common cup of the blood of Christ is dangerous. Not because it will make us sick but because it will make us fit: fit to suffer and fit to celebrate. Fit for communion with each other and for union with a God who not only changes wine into blood but also sorrow into joy, orphans into offspring, strangers into sisters and brothers. How? Why?

The answers lie in the action. What does it mean to take this cup, drink from it and share in it? The common cup is a sign, a source of common destiny: We are in this together. We live in Christ together. We belong to God now, and that belonging is manifested in the commitment that we have to each other. There is no escaping the fundamental reality that we live no longer for ourselves but with and for one another. What happens to you happens to me. And even more so, it happens to us. Taking up and drinking from this cup, we pledge our lives to Christ by pledging our lives to one another. The taking and the drinking and the sharing of the one cup makes us one.

That is why it has never been the Catholic, Lutheran, Anglican or Orthodox practice to give each person a separate cup. We cannot do that because we know that this is about more than (but never less than) "me and Jesus." This is about Christ and us, Christ and the church. The single loaf is torn to pieces, ripped to shreds so that all may eat. And it's easy — especially when our lack of fervor leads us to the eminently practical but impoverished practice of using hundreds of self-contained minia-ture wafers — to think that Jesus is mine and I am his, and the rest of you don't figure into this. But if the fracturing of the loaf allows us to overlook that the bread was one, and that now we are one body, the common cup will not let us forget: We die and we rise in community. Grapes only grow in bunches, and wine was never made from a solitary grape. Suffering is shared by all the members of this body, and your joy, my joy is magnified when it becomes our joy.

For this is a cup of both suffering and joy, of both pain and promise. This is the bitter cup that Jesus begged be taken from him, but the cup that he nonetheless accepted and drank from before taking up the cross. By taking up this cup, we take up the cross! Wine is made by smashing grapes, literally by stomping the life out of them. The blood of the grapes is strained and puri-fied and entombed in oak barrels. And then the miracle: Lifeless liquid ferments. What was bland is now tart and flavorful. What would go down as easy as water now inebriates.

This is the cup that Jesus offers us: The cup of death-turned-into-life, the chalice of sorrow-fermented-into-giddy-joy. Is this not what all people thirst for — what we thirst for? Can I afford to pass it up? How can we die to the self without accept-ing this chalice, without pouring our own passions and pains into the passion and pain of Christ? (Without the paschal mystery, our own suffering is sadly meaningless.) How can we rise to com-munion without drinking from this cup, without spiking our own bland joy with the ferment of Christ's resurrection? (Without the paschal mystery, our own joy is illusory and fleeting.) What other cup, what other drink, can satisfy our thirst? There is a potency

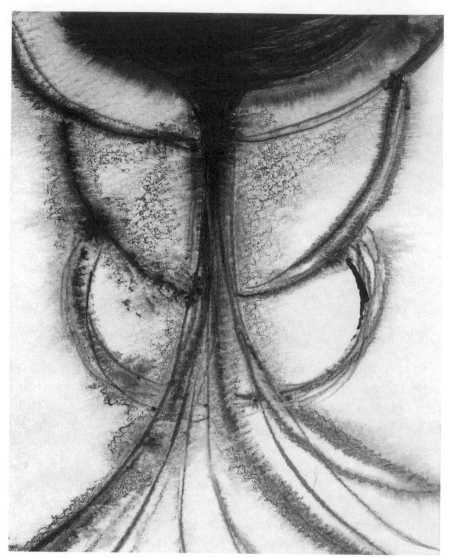

here in this common cup and without it we cannot live — or afford to die. And if we are not thirsty for what this cup contains, then something is wrong. If we do not thirst for communion, with Christ and with each other, then we have not heard the gospel or worked hard enough at living its life.

There is more. This cup is thanksgiving; this wine, our gratitude. Reborn of water and the Holy Spirit, giving thanks is in our blood; we live to be grateful. How do we practice gratitude? How do we give thanks? By taking up this cup, in faith.

Because God is so gracious, we know that if we must pass this cup up on occasion — because of a cold or because we cannot safely take alcohol — Christ still comes to us whole and entire under the sign of bread alone. But for most of us, most of the time, we must live true to what the psalmist has us sing:

What gift can ever repay
God's gift to me?
I raise the cup of freedom
as I call on God's name!
I fulfill my vows to you, Lord,
standing before your assembly.
—Psalm 116:12–14

And why? The psalmist sings the answer:

Death had me in its grip,
the grave's trap was set,
grief held me fast.
I cried out for God,
"Please, Lord, rescue me."

God rescues me from death,
wiping my tears,
steadying my feet.
I walk with the Lord
in this land of the living.
—Psalm 116:3–4, 8–9

Singing these words, let us go to the table, bearing gifts of bread and wine. And humbly, in faith, let us raise the cup of freedom. "Take this, all of you, and drink from it. This is the cup of my blood, the blood of the new and everlasting covenant. It will be shed for you and for all so that sins may be forgiven. Do this in memory of me."

BLESS US, O LORD, AND THESE THY GIFTS

So much more is fed at the table than hunger and thirst! Early science fiction portrayed taking a meal as obsolete: A whole dinner was distilled into a pill that Captain Kirk swallowed in a second. It saved him time and gave him all the necessary nutrients—more than food and drink might have. It even gave him the tastes of turkey and gravy, cranberry sauce, sweet potatoes and green beans, and red wine, filling his stomach to satisfaction.

But as efficient as this dinner pill was, something was lacking. Maybe that's why later science fiction did away with it: Aboard the next generation's starship *Enterprise,* Captain Picard ordered up real grub. Sure, it was computer generated (made in the "food replicator"), but it was food that had to be chewed and drink ("Tea—Earl Grey—hot!") that had to be sipped at the table. That led to more frequent dinner scenes in the sequel series, like those intimate breakfasts with Doctor Beverly Crusher. So much more is fed at the table than hunger and thirst.

How is it in your household? We don't quite have meal pills, but with drive-through hot dog stands and transportable tacos, we can habitually eat on the run and avoid eating at the table or with others. Maybe that's our ironic obedience of the command given to the Israelites: "This is how you shall eat . . . with your loins girded, your sandals on your feet and your staff in hand; and you shall eat . . . hurriedly" (Exodus 12:11). No. We know that we truly lack something if we forego the table, skip the formality, avoid others and simply ingest. So much more is fed at the table than hunger and thirst.

The Gaelic word for family can be translated literally as "those who eat together." A "companion" is literally someone with whom you share bread. And if you have ever had the experience of being seated at a table with a complete stranger in a busy restaurant, you know that some of the uncomfortableness comes from the fact that eating together implies some kind of connection that in this case you don't have. The sharing of food and drink is really the sharing of lives: stories told between mouthfuls and advice passed with the pepper. Eating and drinking together creates and sustains communion.

But even for those who live alone, eating at the table is different from eating on the run. It requires putting aside other occupations, clearing off the table's top, setting out the utensils. And if you can resist the temptation to read or watch television, eating at the table can be an opportunity to savor food and drink and peace, and be refreshed. So much more is fed at the table than hunger and thirst.

And so we turn to God and pray at the table before eating and drinking. The food and drink is itself a gift from our provident God, the first farmer, who sowed the forests and planted the prairies and husbanded all the animals and stocked the seas; the ancient gardener who planted Eden. That would be reason enough to pause and say thank you, and yet there is more.

Not only is the food and drink a gift from the God who provides; the eating and the drinking is an encounter with the God who liberates. On the eve of the Exodus, what did God command the people to do? Pack their bags? Take out traveler's insurance? No. The Living God gave Israel a menu, including a recipe for lamb, and commanded them to eat dinner carefully. And in that meal, a new people was born — the community of those passed over by the angel of death, the community of those who would walk dry-footed through tempestuous seas and wet-lipped through dusty deserts.

Eating and drinking is a way to be with God! Jesus knew this. No wonder the authorities accused him of being a glutton — he was always eating and drinking with people! And because Jesus understood that God is the so-much-more on which we feed at our tables, he made the meal the vehicle of his sacrifice and risen presence. Here, at this holy table, we obey his command: "Eat and drink in memory of me." But not only here, also at home: When we take our daily bread at our own tables, we remember Christ. And our daily bread is made holy and our daily cup is consecrated, and our own tables become altars

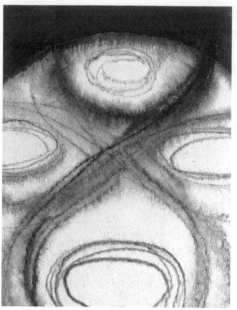

where God sits down with us. Imagine it!

We lift up our hearts to God here, around the church's table, the Lord's table, because we learn to do so at home, around the kitchen table and the dining room table. We give thanks and praise to God here, over this bread and wine, because we learn to give thanks and praise at home, over spaghetti and spinach, coffee and cola.

So lift up your plate and your cup at home. And whether you live alone or with others, raise your eyes to heaven and say, "Bless us, O Lord, and these your gifts, which we are about to receive, from your bounty, through Christ our Lord. Amen." If you do, if we all do, our hearts will be true when we lift up this bread and raise this cup in the memory of the one who called us here, the one who loved us to the death and more.

Then can we leave this table liberated from death. Then can we leave our own tables each day with the heart's hunger both fed and deepened and the soul's thirst both satisfied and increased. Then can we become food and drink for a world longing for a taste of love and a sip of the life that never dies.

WALK ALWAYS

A throng of persons walking on a crowded city street is precisely that—a coincidental collection of individuals who happen to be moving in the same direction. But when those individuals move in the same direction for a common purpose—to end a war, to demand civil rights, to celebrate a victory or to remember a hero—the act of walking unites them. A pace and a rhythm emerge that form the throng into an assembly. And should that assembly begin to shout syncopated slogans or to sing, it raises one voice. Walking and singing together unite a group of individuals into a body, an assembly, a people.

So it is at liturgy. If singing an opening song unites the members of the assembly into one voice, walking in procession unites us into one body. (This is why processions often are gathering rituals.) Certainly, the processions that we make have their uses: The entrance procession moves the ministers from the door to the center of the assembly; the gospel procession moves the book through the assembly to the ambo; the procession of the catechumens moves them from this room to the chapel; the gifts procession carries the money, the bread and the wine to the altar; the communion procession moves us from our places to the table; the final procession takes us from this liturgy back to the world. But besides these functions, our processions have significance; they mean something, and they do something to us.

Walking and singing in procession teaches us in our skin and bones what it means to be human, what it means to be a Christian assembly, what it means to have the new Jerusalem as our destination and destiny. Walking and singing in procession makes us human, *unites* us as an assembly and puts us on the road to the new Jerusalem.

Think about the processions at Sunday Mass. The liturgy begins in motion. People gather and converge. The music begins. The cross is lifted up and moves forward. And we follow. We follow the cross; we go where it goes. We carry with us our book, held high overhead. We move into this room singing, and though the words we sing vary from week to week with the seasons of the year, any songs that we sing are really only echoes of the psalm:

> Enter the temple gates,
> the courtyard with thanks and praise;
> give thanks and bless God's name.
> —Psalm 100:4

All of us "process" from home to here, but most often only the ministers actually walk the procession. That's too bad. It's too bad that we deem it impractical for all of us to actually walk and sing in procession, to do in ritual what we have done in practice: enter—in our bodies, as a body—into this liturgy. We look for and find and follow the cross out there every day of our baptized lives; it would be good for all of us to do so here, in ritual.

The same is true of the gospel procession. Aren't we commissioned to carry the good news? Don't we carry the gospel of Christ's dying and rising in our hearts every day, everywhere, every way? When the time comes, the deacon or priest carries this large, lovely book through the assembly. Why? The gospel is dynamic, never static. It moves us as it moves among us. The gospel moves.

When that book passes by your pew, don't you want to jump out into the aisle and follow it? Don't you want to walk the way of the word, stand around Christ, hear the good news and then move on to live it out? Maybe in our ritual we should do what we try to do in our daily living: Follow the gospel, carry it here and there, go where it leads us.

In some parishes, instead of passing baskets to collect money for the poor and for the church, people leave their seats and form a procession. They come to the altar, walking through clouds of incense pouring from vessels held by servers. They leave their gift of money or canned goods in baskets and present themselves as gifts by way of bowing to the altar. In other parishes, a few representatives of the assembly carry the bread and the wine and the money in procession.

There is one procession at Mass that all of us do make—the communion procession. How important it is to walk and sing this way! When we walk and sing the communion procession, we are struggling to begin the communion that Christ perfects in us. This body, lifting up one song with one voice, flows to the one altar, shares the one loaf (broken into pieces) and drinks from the one cup (poured out into many). This is communion: to be one body, one spirit with each other, with Christ, with God.

Processions ritualize what human life on earth is — a sojourn, a pilgrimage. The metaphor "life is a journey" is a cliché, but it is nonetheless true. Like Abraham and Sarah, we set out for a place to which God calls us. Like the Israelites who passed dry-shod through the sea into the desert, we pass through this earthly life only for a time. Like Jeremiah, we embark carrying a word that sometimes makes us flinch. Like Isaiah, we climb God's mountain path to see the other side. Like the beloved in

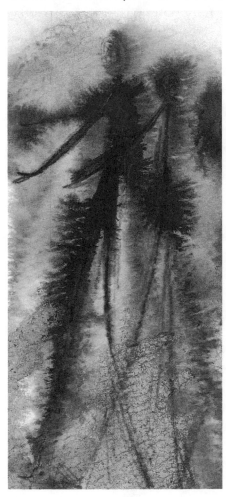

the Song of Songs, we walk the streets looking for the one whom we love. Like Ruth, we glean the fields for a few grains of nourishment. Like the itinerant Christ, we go from place to place carrying good news, and we walk the way of tears. Like the faithful women, we march to the tomb to face death, then run from there in amazement. Like Magdalene, we hurry to others with life-changing news. Like the pentecostal apostles, we spill out of our hiding place into the streets to both bring and seek the One who lives.

For those who are baptized, life is a procession, a progress through times and places, a march through experiences of dying to self and rising in love. The poet Antonio Machado wrote, *"Caminante, no hay camino/se hace camino al andar."* ("Walker, there is no road/the road is made by walk-ing.") That's why the liturgy depends so much on processions to move it along: Jesus is the way to live, and the only way to find the way is to walk and sing it.

The direction in which the baptized move is toward the new Jerusalem, that heavenly city of peace built by divine-human cooperation where no one will be homeless, hungry or hopeless. That's where we need to go. When we were baptized, we were given a candle lit from the paschal candle — that lovely image of the risen Christ. And we were told this:

> You have been enlightened by Christ.
> Walk always as a child of the light
> and keep the flame of faith alive in your heart.
> When the Lord comes, may you go out to meet him
> with all the saints in the heavenly kingdom.

And we responded, "Amen," that is, "so be it." Every procession that we undertake after that procession to the font and through the waters is a rehearsal for the ultimate one that will lead us to the new Jerusalem. For when our days on earth are over, and our bodies sleep in the Lord, those we leave behind will carry our bodies on their final procession from funeral parlor to church to grave. Meanwhile every procession that we undertake inches us closer to home.

SINGING IN THE ASSEMBLY

When we come to this assembly, we are asked to do something that we are seldom (if ever) asked to do elsewhere. Some of us find it a difficult request — we think that we are not capable. Or we think that it is something that only women (if we are men) or children (if we are adults) or professionals (if we are not) should do. Some of us don't even think about it at all; we simply don't do it out of habit. When we come to this assembly, we are asked, we are expected, to *sing* this liturgy together. And yet, too many of us don't.

Maybe it's difficult for us to sing in here because we don't sing out there much any more. And this is ironic. Our culture is flooded with music. Music from the radio wakes many of us each day. We hear it when we make breakfast, listen to it when we wash and dress. It rides in the car with us on the way to work or school, paces our dash down the aisle of the grocery store, squeezes into the elevator with us, answers the phones of the businesses that we call — it's even piped into some bathrooms! Music is part of the background noise of modern life.

And if we are unaware of it most of the day, there are times when we listen to it on purpose: We sit to relax with the stereo headphones and a favorite album. What would a party be without music? Household chores would be too much drudgery without Sills or Sinatra, Coltrane or Crouche, Beethoven or Brooks, or anybody crooning "Wind Beneath My Wings." And is it even possible to do physics homework without Green Day blaring or to write an essay without the help of Smashing Pumpkins?

Music is very much a part of our culture. But notice how: We *listen* to it, we don't often *make* it. How many of us know how to play an instrument? (And the complicated stereo equipment in our homes doesn't count!) When was the last time that you sang in public? (Did you join in singing the national anthem at the game, or did the performer so "stylize" it that you couldn't join in?) When was the last time that you sang at home? (Did everyone join in "Happy Birthday"? Everyone? How comfortable was that?)

Yet when we come to this assembly, we are required to *make* music, to *make* joyful noises to God — more than the clinking of coins in the collection basket or the murmur of friends conversing after the liturgy ends! The primary mode of music in the liturgy is that which is made by human voices — singing. And not just *some* human voices — as valuable as the ministry of the choir is, the liturgy's primary song is that of this assembly, this whole body, all of us together, the one body of Christ giving voice to the depths of its heart.

Why? Why is it important that we sing in this assembly? That *all* of us sing the parts that belong to all of us — the acclamations, psalms and hymns? What does it mean to sing in the assembly? To sing to and for God?

If you have ever been so moved by the beauty of a meteor streaking across the night sky, the just-opened eyes of a newborn or the touch of one you love so very much, then you know that some things simply cannot be said.

Some experiences are too deep for words alone: Joy, grief, love, tragedy and praise well up inside us and demand to be voiced. What mother does not sing a lullaby? How can Jews who have lost a relative not sing *Kaddish?* In small African villages, as one by one the villagers die of AIDS, why does no one need to coax the living into singing the traditional laments? And are you truly in love with one to whom you never sing a love song, no matter how out of tune?

Words wed to music, sung from the heart, give voice to the deepest human mysteries. And in giving voice to grief or to joy, to love and to praise, we actually deepen our own experience of them. When we are sad and we sing a sad song, we may begin to cry; we certainly mourn more soulfully. When we are overjoyed and sing a joyful song, the joy is made stronger, deeper and wider.

This is one reason why we sing at liturgy — both to express and to deepen praise. Think of the acclamations that we sing, strange and simple words set to music: Amen. Alleluia. Holy, holy, holy. To *speak* these words is somehow deficient. (So much so that the church has a rule: When the assembly does not sing Alleluia, it does not say it either. Better to skip it than to speak it limply.) But when we *sing* these words, the praise that they contain bubbles up and out, and the words ring true. And even if I do not *feel* like praising God right now, if I join in singing "Holy, holy, holy," with the rest of God's people, the singing nonetheless carries my heart heavenward. Singing together not only does something inside me and you, but it also does something for us as a body. It unites us. If you were to stand outside this room as the entrance hymn is sung, you would be able to tell whether it's a large group or a small group doing the singing. But you would not be able to tell with certainty how many voices are singing. One voice is lifted up in song, and that is precisely why we begin all our liturgies with singing. The singing makes us one. The body Christ—many though its members—lifts up one voice to God, the very voice of Christ.

And so it is with the communion song. The singing and the walking and the eating and the drinking, done together, help create the communion—the union that we share with each other through, with and in Christ. There's no delicate way of saying this: If you do not sing as you come to the table, if you do not at least make the effort to join in the song, you come to this table a freeloader. You're not carrying your weight, not doing your part, not offering your praise, not saying "Thank you." You're muting the voice of the body of Christ. So give voice to Christ: Sing as you come to this table. The church needs you to join in the song; we are all the weaker if you don't.

Not only as we enter into the liturgy, not only when we go to the table—we also sing in all other processions that we make. It's natural: Singing while walking gives us a pace, a rhythm with which to move. Military cadets in training often sing as they jog. It regulates breathing; it syncopates the actions of a bunch of individuals into the movement of a corps; it sets a pace and gives the activity a sound and a flavor and a feel that it otherwise would not have.

As we Christians move through our liturgy, we sing. As we move through our communal life, we sing. We sing when we meet the infants and the catechumens at the door, to welcome them in and give them a place at the foot of the ambo so that they can hear God's word. We sing when the bride and the groom enter the assembly to make their vows. We sing when the body of a dead sister or brother is brought inside the church for the last time.

And we sing through the seasons of the year, too. What would Advent be like without "O come, o come, Emmanuel" or Christmas without the carols? Would it truly be Easter without the chanting of the Exsultet or without the glad sounds of "Jesus Christ is ris'n today"? Would we know the Spirit's presence on Pentecost if we forgot to sing "Come, Holy Ghost"?

To give voice to the deepest experiences of our hearts, to give voice to the body of Christ, to unite us, to move us through our rites, our life, our seasons, we need to sing in this assembly. We need to sing in here, so that perhaps we can learn to sing again out there, to sing together in a world ironically cacophonous with noise yet a world in which the poor and the oppressed still do not have a voice, still have little reason to sing. Perhaps if we practice singing in here, we will be better able to start a few choruses out there: songs of protest as well as praise; songs of real need that expose the lie in the jingles of advertised want; songs of the true joy that is found when people live together, sing together, in harmony.

And if you are tempted to think that singing together is useless, remember what happened when South Africans sang, in ever-increasing numbers, the banned anthem of a free South Africa; or what happened when Poles joined voices to sing of Solidarity; or what happened when African Americans lifted every voice to sing "We shall overcome." Singing together will change us. We have only to take up the tune.

RISE LIKE INCENSE

"No Smoking." There's a sign of the times—literally. We've come to learn how unhealthy smoking tobacco is, and now more and more people struggle against nicotine addiction, even as some devious money-grubbers continue to entice teenagers into the habit.

"Holy smokes!" our grandparents might have exclaimed. But we have seen in this century some of the most evil smoke that human beings have ever created: pouring from the ovens at Auschwitz, Bergen-Belsen, Dachau and other Nazi camps; blotting out the skies of London and Pearl Harbor; spewing from the fireball that consumed Dresden; ballooning like a grotesque mushroom from the ruins of Hiroshima and Nagasaki; eating up test islands in the Pacific. And in our own country, we have seen the sad and costly smoke of racism as our cities burned: Watts in Los Angeles, the inner city of Detroit, the Madison Street corridor in Chicago, parts of Harlem and the South Bronx in New York City. We have breathed the poisonous smoke belched from industry's stacks. Then the jobs that produced it were taken away suddenly, and it was dreams and homes and histories that went up in smoke. *Holy* smokes?

But yes. There is smoke that is holy: the nontoxic clouds that rise from busy factories that work tirelessly to be clean; the tendrils that climb to the stars from the campfire around which sits a family or a family of friends; the smell of barbecued burgers, ribs and roasted marshmallows hanging under the canopy of the maple in the yard. Such smoke can be holy. Such smoke can act like the pillar of cloud that led Israel in its exodus, leading us to see—no, leading us to smell—the presence of the extraordinary in the ordinary.

My prayers rise before you like incense, O God. Is it any wonder that when they built their Temple to the invisible, inscrutable God, our Jewish ancestors burned incense daily to accompany their prayers of petition and praise? What better way to attract the attention and arouse the compassion of the God who was as elusive to the senses as a whiff of perfume yet as powerful to save as a pillar of fire and cloud? And what better way to show love for such a God than by taking something so precious, so full of the promise of pleasure, and burn it—all for God's sheer delight? Who in Jerusalem was not moved to see the Temple on the hill, smoke pouring out of its courtyards, filling the city with sweetness? Entering the Temple courts, wouldn't the sight and smell of sweet smoke floating through shafts of sunlight be an irresistible invitation to pray?

We, too, honor God by incensing this assembly, this book, this table. Our hearts go up in smoke! We fill this room with the fog of prayer at dawn as we sing Zechariah's blessing and again at dusk when we chant Mary's Magnificat. We raise the bread and wine on waves of incense. We swirl in sweet smoke the bride and the groom. We send up the souls of the dead on clouds of perfume. Always before the cross go the ephemeral curls of frankincense and myrrh, cedar and sage and pine. (They beckon us to follow.) This holy smoke carries our cries upward, raises up our praise, purifies the air of sin and sorrow. It dances delightfully above our heads and waltzes into our nostrils, filling our lungs with thanksgiving. It puts petitions on our lips; we pray for the world like Christ. We rise like incense!

Let my prayers come before you like incense, O God, and the lifting up of my hands like an evening sacrifice. When one of our Christian foremothers was dragged before the procurator for treason, she was offered a way out: If she burned incense before the image of Caesar, she could go home. But her emperor was Christ, not Caesar; her allegiance was to the coming reign of God, a reign that put the lie to *Pax Romana,* the rule of the rich. She kicked the brazier over, sending up a spray of sparks. Later, at the stake, her own flesh turned to smoke, an offering of self that reached to heaven.

Burning incense is political. To whom do we offer our homage, our hearts? Burning incense before Christ's cross *here,* we promise to kick over any brazier erected to perfume the powerful or honor the honored *out there.* Burning incense before this assembly, this book, this table *here,* we promise to resist and reform any system *out there* that lets a few bathe in expensive

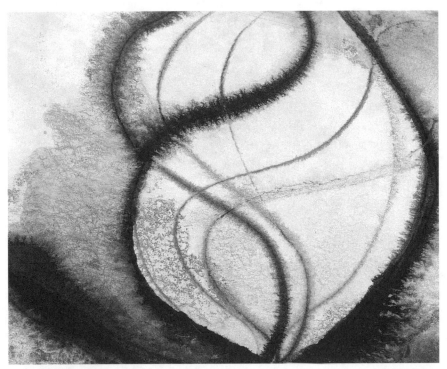

colognes while others stink in putrid poverty. Burning incense *here,* we vow to burn up energy *out there,* so that the whole world rises like incense to God, and poverty is changed to perfume by the fire of our love.

What happens is that the perfume, trapped within the hardened kernels of resin, is set free when tossed on the ember. These hard grains are odorless until softened by heat and melted by fire. Then sweetness escapes its solid prison and floats free, filling the air with joy. So it is with the world. Love and justice are trapped in hardened hearts. But the ember of prayer and the Spirit's fire melts hard hearts, opens them up to the suffering of the world and helps them to rise, rise to the cries, rise to the skies, rise like incense.

My prayers, my cries, my praise, my heart, my soul and my body rise like incense before you, O God, the lifting up of my life, this sacrifice.

GO UP WITH JOY

Think about how you came to be here today. Do you usually come to this Mass? Or did you just "pop in"? What were you doing before you came here today? What did you do to prepare: Did you read the scriptures? Put your money in your envelope? Gather canned goods for the food pantry? Pray? Shower? Fast? Don't ask these questions to induce guilt or to set for yourself unrealistic expectations. This much is true: You are here at this Mass; we are here at this Mass; Christ is here at this Mass — it is good for us to be here, however we came to be here.

And it's also good to think about *how* we come to be here each week. Giving thanks and praise to God requires a certain sense of being deliberate, of acting intentionally, with firm purpose. That's hard for us to do today. We live in a very fluid world. Life is now "open 24 hours a day, 7 days a week." We work in shifts. We have cars that make it convenient for us to run errands by allowing us to range far and wide; but that convenience seems to make us even busier: "Let's see, if I drop Maria off at soccer practice, I can take Miguel to his friend's. Then I can pick up a few groceries, go to the mall, stop by church and catch the 12:15, fill the car with gas, and be back home in time to. . . ."

That Mass fits conveniently into a busy schedule is not a bad thing; the practice of our faith needs to be integrated with the whole of our lives. But because this eucharist is something more than just another thing to do on a long list of things to do, because this eucharist is a celebration of paschal mystery, because this eucharist is "necessary and helpful for our salvation," we need to come to Mass with a certain mindfulness, a particular wholeheartedness. Cultivating such a mindfulness and wholeheartedness requires discipline, establishing a routine that will lead us (in mind, heart and body) to enter together into this encounter with the living God that we call eucharist.

Our tradition offers us three ways of preparing for Mass: fasting, washing and dressing. And the times in which we live suggest a few more.

We used to have to abstain from food and drink from Saturday midnight until after we received communion. But Pope Paul VI shortened the fast before communion to one hour. That was a pastoral gesture making it easier for more people (the elderly, those on medication or with special dietary needs) to share in the body and blood of Christ; Christ warned us about putting undue burdens on each other. The hour is a minimum; if you can fast longer, do it. The idea is that we come to this feast hungry — hungry for community, for the word of God, for the sacrificial meal. If we approach this table hungry, we can sing with heightened honesty the ancient communion hymn, Psalm 34: "Taste and see the goodness of the Lord." And we can sing most sincerely to God: "*You* satisfy the hungry heart."

And perhaps we need to fast before Mass from more than food. Maybe our mouths also need to fast from chatting and our tongues from talking. Maybe our eyes need to fast from television, and our ears from the radio. Maybe our hands need to fast from all activities except that which is essential to our — or someone else's — well-being. Maybe our feet need to fast from running errands.

Why? So we come to this assembly mindful, whole-hearted, at peace and ready to participate. Then here we can feast our eyes on the beauty of this gathered people in this place, our noses on the smell of incense, fresh bread and wine, our ears on the notes of organ, piano and guitar, our mouths on songs of praise, our hands on deeds of love, our feet on the dancing that we call "processions."

Washing is another way of preparing for Mass; it's something that we all probably do without thinking. But perhaps the Saturday night or Sunday morning bath or shower can be done with greater care—and a sense of gratitude. Our bodies are temples of the Holy Spirit, members of the body of Christ. We can show great respect for God by caring for our own bodies and for the bodies of the bedridden in our households. What a gift it is to be able to bathe in a tub of hot, sudsy water. What a luxury it is to be able to stand beneath a stream of clean, warm water until we are soaked through. What a reminder of our baptism! Perhaps the bath or shower on Saturday night or Sunday morning can be done more slowly, so as to appreciate it. Perhaps this is the time each week to take a good look at our own bodies and to check for lumps, monitor our weight and attend to our health and hygiene. We do this not to be self-indulgent or vain but to take good care of these temples of the Spirit, these bodies that belong to Christ.

After washing, we dress. What we wear not only says something about how we think and feel about that which we are doing, but it helps us, it makes us think and feel certain things. Imagine going to a ballgame without wearing your favorite team's cap or jersey! Do you go trick-or-treating without a costume? Something would be missing—not right. Wearing clothes may be practical, but what we wear is part of ritual. (That's why our ministers and even this building and our altar wear ritual clothing—vesture, banners and tablecloth.)

All of this is done not to promote some kind of stuffy formality nor to suggest that only the well-dressed and well-heeled are welcome here. Christ may very well show up in this assembly some Sunday, filthy and dressed in rags, and we would not scorn Christ for it. But ask yourself: What is the best way for you to dress in order to participate mindfully and wholeheartedly in this liturgy? And remember, you dress not only for yourself but for us, too. We enjoy you looking your best.

Besides fasting, washing and dressing, many Christians try to read the scriptures before coming to Mass, so as not to hear them at Mass for the first time. That's a fine idea. Another way to do this is to hear the scriptures deliberately each week first at Mass, then keep reading them over and over again during the week, after you've heard the homily. Rereading last week's gospel before hearing this week's will help, especially in Ordinary Time when we read from the gospel somewhat continuously.

And simple recollection can be a useful way of preparing to celebrate Mass. Ask yourself: What am I particularly thankful for this Sunday? What good have I done, what good has society achieved this week that I can offer up to God along with the bread? What pain and sorrow along with the wine? And we never think only of ourselves here. By baptism, we share in Jesus' priesthood, and we, too, stand before God on behalf of the world. The general intercessions are precisely that—general. We add to those general prayers the particular names and places and situations that we know.

If we do these things, we will come to this celebration mindful of God's wonder, wholeheartedly grateful and ready to participate fully in this saving deed. And the words of the psalm will be our own:

> With joy I heard them say,
> "Let us go to the Lord's house!"
> And now, Jerusalem,
> we stand within your gates.
>
> Jerusalem, the city so built
> that city and temple are one.
> To you the tribes go up,
> every tribe of the Lord.
> —Psalm 122:1–4

I AM THE GATE

How many times a day do you pass through a door? Think about it. Think of the door to your home. What does it "do"? It separates outside from inside, sheltering you from the weather, shielding you from the world. It welcomes visitors and keeps back strangers. Open it, and you invite people in; close it, and you provide privacy. How does it look? Is it welcoming or foreboding? Is it solid or pierced with a window? How does it feel? Is it easy to open and close, or does it stick shut or creep ajar on its own? What does it "mean"? The door to your home means that *here* is not *there:* Inside is my home; outside is the rest of the world. But *here* and *there,* home and world, are connected by this door, not completely walled off from each other. And life can be understood as a series of comings and goings, of openings and closings, a process of welcoming in and shutting out, of keeping in and letting out. A door creates and marks a *threshold,* the in-between place, the boundary, the imaginary line that we sometimes cross unthinkingly ("Hurry, you'll miss the bus; I'll get the door!") or sometimes quite deliberately ("If you walk out that door now, don't come back!").

As in our own homes, so, too, is it in the house of the church: The church door shelters and shields, gathers us in and keeps some out (although never, we hope, for the wrong reasons). It creates the threshold between worship and world, between the harvest house and the field farmed. It's the point where these things meet and communicate, the place of entering and the place of going forth, the point both of landing and of launching. And although a door is a door—a practical necessity, a functional device—*this* door, the *church* door, is also more.

Think of what happens at this door. We meet the unbaptized at the door. "What is your name?" we ask in the ritual. "What do you seek?" They (or their godparents) answer and then we lead them inside and offer them a seat to listen to God's word. Not yet baptized, they literally were "outside the church." Through baptism, God brings them inside. Baptism is the door to the house of sacraments; baptism opens the door that swings between worship and world, liturgy and mission.

And then we spend the rest of our lives coming in and going out. Sunday after Sunday, during feasts and fasts, we come in to give God thanks and praise. Nourished by word and sacrament, we then go forth to love and serve the Lord by loving and serving others. The door is the threshold of this interaction, the place where we meet each other coming and going.

And so our processions begin at this door: Here we greet each other as Christ. Here the ministers line up with cross and candles, incense and book. Here the bride and the groom welcome all to the nuptial feast and take their first steps together. And here the bodies of the dead are welcomed back, clothed in the pall that evokes the baptismal gown and sprinkled with holy water for the last time.

On the day of dedication, the church of bone and breath gathers outside the door of the church of brick and board. After a few words, a key is given to the bishop, who opens the door and leads the church in for the first time, saying: "Go within God's gates giving thanks; enter God's courts with songs of praise." And the church sings: "Stretch toward heaven, you gates, open high and wide. Let the glorious sovereign enter."

These actions hallow this door and make it a sacred sign. The door is a sign of baptism. The door is a sign of mission. The door is a sign of Christ: "I am the gate," Jesus says. "Whoever enters by me will be saved, and will come in and go out and find pasture." For us, this door can be the gate of heaven. In order to point clearly to the mystery of baptism, the mystery of mission, the mystery of Christ and the reign of God, the church door must be beautiful and significant. It must be appealing to the eye and delightful to the hand.

When it is the best door that we can provide, when it is lovely, when it reveals the skill of artist and artisan in its design and construction, when it is pulled and pushed for generations by countless hands of the baptized, then our church door points to the life to come. Here then is what we read in the last book of our Bible:

After this I looked, and there in heaven a door stood open! And the first voice, which I heard speaking to me like a trumpet, said, "Come up here. . . ." At once I was in the spirit, and there in heaven stood a throne, with one seated on the throne! Around the throne, and on each side of the throne, are four living creatures. Day and night without ceasing they sing,
   "Holy, holy, holy, the Lord God the Almighty,
   who was and is and is to come."
—Revelation 4:1, 2, 6, 8

And in the creaking and the squeaking of the church door, we can hear Jesus say, "Listen! I am standing at the door, knocking; if you hear my voice and open the door, I will come in to you and eat with you and you with me."

ENTER WITH THANKS AND PRAISE

Remember the first day of school? Did you stand outside for a minute before entering, nervous perhaps, proceeding only after taking a gulp? Remember the last time you went into the grocery store? Probably not. Sometimes we walk into a familiar building—our workplace, the bank—without thinking about it, without even realizing that we've come in from outside.

This happens sometimes when we come into the church's house, too. Maybe we're running a little late, we missed the bus or couldn't find a place to park, so we rush in and take the closest seat. Or maybe some of us, with something akin to the first day of school jitters, come in, feel a little self-conscious and try to slide quickly into the seat farthest from the altar but closest to the door.

In so doing, sometimes we neglect some old habits—some old but good manners that many of us were taught as children. What do you do when you enter a home? You're welcomed in. A dialogue of hellos and introductions follows. You meet strangers and greet any guests of honor. You find a good place to sit or stand. You join in the conversation and activity.

When we enter this house, the church's house, in one sense, no one who is baptized and no one who is a catechumen is a guest here: God's house is the church's house; we are at home here. In another sense, we are all guests here: No one comes here unless called here by God. And like entering any house, entering the house of the church has some rituals that help us enter truly into the conversation and the activity that goes on in here—the liturgy.

As a sign of the hospitality of the reign of God, we establish the ministry of ushers to greet us as we come through the door. But hospitality is not their responsibility alone: We should greet each other as we would greet Christ. It doesn't matter whether we are friends in a social sense. A simple smile and nod and maybe a "hello" all serve to acknowledge that one of the ways we find Christ in this place is in each other.

At the door, we bless ourselves with the water of baptism, "holy water." Today, we think of this gesture as a reminder that it is by virtue of our baptism that we enter this room to do this deed, to do the liturgy. That's a fine interpretation. The historical fact is that the Jews, our spiritual ancestors, washed their hands (and sometimes their feet, too!) before they prayed, as do Moslems and Hindus and some Buddhists. Perhaps it was once a real scrubbing, but by the time of Jesus it was a ceremony that had taken on spiritual significance: One must be purified to pray to God. And Jesus was quick to teach his followers that the heart must be cleansed more so than the hands.

So when you come into this room, bless yourself with water. Remember that baptism cleansed you and renewed you. Resolve to enter into this liturgy with a pure heart. Look to the altar, sign yourself with a watery cross and know that the journey to this table began at the tub, the baptismal font that was the tomb for your old self and the womb that gave birth to a child of God and member of this body of Christ: you!

And when you find a place, bow to the altar before taking a seat. Don't just nod your head: Bow deeply, gracefully from the waist. Recognize Christ in this sign: a dining table, sitting in the shadow of the cross, the shade of the tree of life; a dining table where God sits with us and heaven comes to earth like a feast comes to those who are starving. When you bow to the altar, you bow to Christ. And not only do you show your love for Christ in our midst, but by your bodily action, you also deepen that love.

Speaking of finding a place, why do we fill up this room from the back to the front? Maybe it's piety: We sit in the back because, aware of our many failings, we don't feel worthy to draw near. Maybe it's culture: We sit in the back because our mothers taught us never to claim the best seats or make ourselves the center of attention. Maybe it's practical: We want to be able to skip out early. Whatever the reason, it causes a problem: The front seats are empty, creating a gulf between the Lord's table and the Lord's people. And latecomers stand in the back rather than march up front, showing everybody that they're late.

Let's show some hospitality here! Let's fill the house of the church up from the front to the back, leaving the back rows for those who come later or late. And let's fill each row from the center: If you're the first one in a row, don't hug the end (unless you're a minister and will need to get in and out). Move to the middle so that others may come and sit beside you.

Filling in the front seats first isn't being proud or arrogant. It's part of the ministry of hospitality that all of us who are baptized (or longing to be baptized) are called to exercise. It's a simple act of kindness that helps the church to gather better around its Lord.

Upon taking your seat, again acknowledge Christ present in the people sitting around you. Introduce yourself if that seems right, but a simple smile and nod are just as good as any chatting. Some people like to kneel and pray. That's a fine custom. In some monasteries, the practice is to stand attentively for a few moments before sitting. We come here because God has called us here, we come as servants. We come to wait upon God's word and to carry it out. Standing attentively for a moment — as if waiting for our orders, as if waiting for God's voice — is a good practice. It helps us to collect ourselves and to realize that taking a seat in this place will demand something more of us than taking a seat in a movie theater or a restaurant demands.

When you sit, prepare your offering for the collection and find the opening song. Resolve yourself to sing it. If you picked up the bulletin or the diocesan paper on the way in, don't read it now; leave it until later.

Some people find it helpful to read scriptures, prayers or other sacred texts as a way of preparing their minds and hearts to enter into the liturgy. That's a fine practice as long as it's not intended to ignore others present and pretend that somehow this liturgy is my time to be alone with Jesus. Being alone with Jesus is a great thing to do every day: Come and spend some time in the tabernacle chapel during the week. But being alone with Jesus is not our purpose in the minutes before Mass begins. We come to Mass to encounter God together, in and with and through Christ; to be the body of Christ, with Jesus as the head and us as the members. Saint Paul warned us:

> Examine yourselves, and only then eat of the bread and drink of the cup. For all who eat and drink *without discerning the body,* eat and drink judgment against themselves.
>
> —1 Corinthians 11:29 – 30

Now of course he was talking about having faith in the mystery of the eucharist and about preparing to make our sacrifice of praise by living just lives. But I think he also could mean that we have to recognize the fact that Christ is present in this gathering of the baptized, as close to you as the person sitting next to you. We need to discern the body of Christ in this assembly, in this parish! If we stick our noses in pious books or bury our faces in our hands to avoid each other, and think that we are therefore being alone with Jesus, we are sadly mistaken.

If we take some care to enter our liturgy by practicing these manners, we may find that we all enter our liturgy with bodies primed for the gestures and postures, with minds focused on the holy work at hand and with hearts more free to give God thanks and praise.

THIS COMMUNITY NOW SENDS YOU FORTH

My dear friends, this community now sends you forth to reflect more deeply upon the word of God which you have shared with us today. Be assured of our loving support and prayers for you. We look forward to the day when you will share fully in the Lord's table.
　　　　—Rite of Christian Initiation of Adults

It seems a bit odd. We make such efforts to welcome people who have not been baptized to join us. After a period of inquiry, we receive them formally into the catechumenate, the "assembly of those who learn through hearing." They stand outside the door, and we go to them in procession. We ask them their names and what they are seeking. We welcome them in and give them certain seats so that, with us, they hear God's word. Then, just as we are about to do the very thing that makes us who we are—just as we are about to respond to God's word by pleading on behalf of the world, by taking up bread and wine, by giving thanks and praise—we ask the catechumens to leave. We send them out.

It seems so odd. Why not let them stay? Why make them wait until baptism before they take their place around the Lord's table with us?

Some argue that it's an archaic practice not worth reviving. We know that the early church held the intercessions and the eucharistic prayer in such regard that no unbaptized person could witness them, not to mention participate in them. This custom was common in other religions of the time, too: The heart of the sacred mysteries was reserved for those who were initiated. The mysteries were secret. But now, 1500 years later, the Christian church has no secrets. The Mass has even been broadcast on television! And besides, some of the catechumens have been coming to church and sitting through the whole Mass for years. So why send them out now?

That objection often is linked to another: Some would argue that life is too short to play games. We want these folks to join us; they've shown interest in joining us. Why not dispense with the ceremony, give them a certificate of membership and be done with it?

These are valid points. Life indeed is too short. We do indeed want these folks to be baptized. But the lengthy process of initiation is no more a game than childhood is a game, than growth is a game, than grieving the death of a loved one is a game. We know that human life is a series of steps: A person is born only after gestating in the womb for nine months; it takes ten to fifteen years to achieve sexual maturity; it takes as long as it takes to stop sobbing and get on with life when someone close has died. We cannot rush these things. Or at least we do so at great risk of losing something of what it means to be human.

What we are doing with these catechumens is as fundamental as giving birth to a baby, as complicated as surviving adolescence and as compelling as caring for someone who is dying. That, in fact, is what happens, although perhaps in a different order. The catechumenate is a hospice in which the Adam and the Eve in each of these individuals is dying. And the catechumenate is a therapist's office where the work of grieving (here it is called repentance) is begun. And the catechumenate is a prenatal clinic, where new life gestating in the womb is cared for and monitored. These things take time.

We dismiss the catechumens after the homily and before the prayers of the faithful because they are at a point in their progress where they need to continue digesting God's word. The early church used a metaphor that may seem condescending today, but it still teaches us something. The metaphor was that catechumens are babies without teeth. Babies without teeth cannot chew bread. So they drink their mothers' milk — the word of

God—until they are ready to eat, and not choke on, solid food—the eucharist.

The metaphor doesn't always work. Far from being "spiritual infants," some of our catechumens are more mature than some of us. But the insight is still good: At different points in life and growth, different things are required. The catechumenate is the restaurant where the word of God is served in heaping portions to be savored. That's the catechumens' need, their duty, their responsibility right now: to eat and drink fully of the scriptures in order to develop an appetite, a taste for the sacrificial meal.

So they are sent forth because they cannot do what we must do after the word has been proclaimed and broken open. Not yet baptized, not yet made into "other Christs," the catechumens cannot stand before the throne and intercede on behalf of the world. We ourselves could not do so if we were not grafted onto Christ, made members of his body by holy baptism. Not yet baptized, the catechumens cannot yet lift up their hearts with Christ, in Christ and through Christ to give thanks and praise to the Father and to call down the Spirit.

This is not a put-down; it is merely a fact. These are things that only Christ can do; and in order to be in Christ, one must be baptized and anointed. Infants are no less valuable because they cannot eat steak. You are no less valuable than the ambassador to China because you cannot sign a treaty. Each of us has different roles to fulfill for the good of all.

Maybe the word "dismiss" confuses us. We are not "dismissing" the catechumens, as we brush off someone with whom we wish to be bothered no longer. Rather, we *send the catechumens* forth to be who they are and to do what they do: to be those who "learn by hearing," by wrestling with the word of God as they discern the road ahead, the road that may lead to the font, and from the font to the table, and from the table to the world. They do not go their separate ways. And they do not go alone. They go together with a catechist, one of us, as a guide.

In order to do as we have done, in order to renounce the devil and profess Christ, they need to know what it is they are getting into, who they are being called to become. In order to do what we do, in order to plead "Lord, hear our prayer" and in

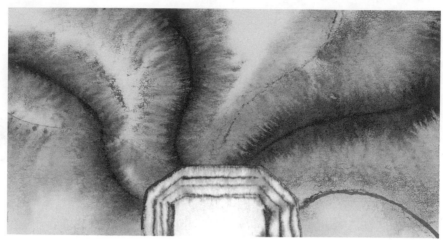

order to sing "It is right to give God thanks and praise!" they need to be born again of water and the Spirit; they need to finish dying so that they can begin living. Let's not rush that. The waiting will be worthwhile, as worthwhile as the months of pregnancy (despite morning sickness and water retention!).

The newly baptized often report that such waiting, such expectancy was an important part of the spiritual path, a custom that groomed a listening heart and a love for the scriptures that will be needed later. For after the bathing and the anointing and the eating and the drinking comes the mission: the life-and-death work of fulfilling the reign of God. For this we must help them prepare. And the preparing begins by drinking deeply of the words that flow from deep inside this book of the scriptures.

GO, YOU ARE SENT

We come here so that we can go from here. It's tempting to think that we come to the liturgy to get away from the world, to have a moment of respite, to "rest a minute with Jesus." And maybe that happens — coincidentally. But the fact is that we come in here to be sent back out there. When Jesus went up Mount Tabor with Peter, James and John and was transfigured, appearing in glory between Moses and Elijah, Peter truly enjoyed the beauty of the moment. "It's good for us be here," he said, "Let's build three tents so that you and Moses and Elijah can stay. Let's savor this glory for awhile." But no sooner had he spoken than the vision dissipated. Jesus' feet were once more touching the ground, treading down Tabor toward Jerusalem, the great city, toward the table and the cross and the tomb. There is a lesson here for us: We come in here to be sent out there.

Think of the very name that we give this liturgy — the Mass. The word "Mass" comes from the Latin word *missa,* one of the last words of the rite: *Ite, missa est.* We hear this translated most often as "Go in peace to love and serve the Lord." More literally, it is "Go, you are sent out." The reason why *Ite, missa est* was first used to end the liturgy is simple. It was a Roman expression used to conclude civic functions or public gatherings. It was used to conclude the liturgy because the liturgy, too, is a civic function and a public gathering. And no song followed this conclusion; when the deacon said "Go, you are sent out," that was the end of it; all left.

Now there are many names for this ritual that we do: liturgy, eucharist, Lord's supper, the breaking of the bread. Why would one of these names be "Mass," or "The Sending Out"? It would be like calling a stage play a "curtain call" or calling a film "the end": "Do you want to go see a curtain call or the end this Friday night?"

No one claims that any meaning is intended here: Our Roman Christian ancestors didn't think this through and do this on purpose. But the meaning is true nonetheless: "Mass" is an appropriate name for this act of worship, because we come in here so that God may send us back out there. Everything that we do in here, we do not only for its own sake but also for the sake of the world.

We gather together here as the church, not to be some mutual admiration society but rather to practice being that all-inclusive community that the world is called to be. We gather together here to be the church *for* the world, to be salt for the earth, light for the world, a city set atop the hill for all to see and enter. We listen together to God's word — not only to be nourished individually but also to be commissioned corporately, to be given our task, our assignment, our role in transforming this world into the reign of God. We take bread and wine and offer thanks and praise and share the body and the blood not just for our own sanctification but for the salvation of the whole world, so "that from east to west a perfect offering may be made to the glory" of God's name. And we share the body and the blood so that we — not only as individuals but more so as a church, a community — can be bread for the hungry and wine for those who thirst.

That's why it makes good sense to call this entire liturgy Mass, "The Sending Out." It's not that we want to rush through our worship and get on to more important things. Instead, we want to take our time with this ritual in order to rehearse carefully in here what it is we are working for out there: a communion of persons where all are welcomed, where the stories that lay bare the meaning of our lives are told and told again, where each and every one has a seat at the table with God. In fact, we should be like Peter, desiring greatly to stay here and enjoy the glory and the beauty of the Mass. But we should be more like Christ, who carried the beauty of the vision with him back into the street, onto the road to Jerusalem, in order to do what he was sent to do: transform death into life.

We did not come here as a random group of strangers. We were summoned here by God in virtue of the water bath and the anointing. We do not leave here a random group of strangers. We are sent out in the power of the Holy Spirit to be the body of Christ at work in the world. We are not sent out alone (the "you" is not a bunch of me's, it's second-person plural; it's us.) We are not sent out empty handed. We go out knowing more clearly who we are. We go out with a fire burning in our souls, with a word on our lips, with nourishment in our bellies. We go out eager to do the work of the one who sends us, fortified to fight evil rather than to flee from it, ready to pass through pain rather than ignore it, resolved to defeat death rather than deny it.

Go, you are sent: to live your life gratefully, to give God thanks always. Go, you are sent: to do your job well. Go, you are sent: to enjoy this life's pleasures and promises. Yes, and even more. Go, you are sent: to heal the earth of polluted waters and poisoned skies. Go, you are sent: to resist the purchase of military armaments with money that could buy milk or books for children. Go, you are sent: to nurture and protect life, from conception to natural death. Go, you are sent: to make sure that the sick have adequate healthcare, regardless of their ability to pay. Go, you are sent: to welcome the immigrant, to embrace the foreigner. Go, you are sent: to forgive the one who has wronged you and to seek forgiveness from those you have wronged. Go, you are sent: to love, and to love some more. Go, you are sent. *You* are sent. You are *sent*. Thanks be to God.

APPENDIX
USING THESE REFLECTIONS

1. With the Lectionary

The following list lets the lectionary suggest suitable chapters to read or preach. When preaching, it's important not to force a connection between the scripture and the topic. In most cases, a word or sentence or image of the scripture evokes the phrase, gesture or object from the liturgy. It may not even be necessary to point that out. Or it may be that the line of scripture can serve as a refrain in preaching.

     Any of the chapters can be used in any order on all the Sundays of Ordinary Time, even when the scriptures are not echoed or evoked. The same is true of the Sundays of the Easter season, the traditional time to preach about the sacred mysteries.

Advent

First Sunday
A Day of the Lord; To Stand in Your Presence; Go Up with Joy
B, C Day of the Lord; Keeping Silence

Second Sunday
A Day of the Lord; Word of the Lord
B Day of the Lord; Word of the Lord; Walk Always
C Go Up with Joy; Enter with Thanks and Praise

Third Sunday
A Keeping Silence; Calling to Mind
B Let Your Spirit; This Community Now Sends You Forth
C Let Us Pray to the Lord; We Bring You These Gifts; Calling to Mind

Fourth Sunday
B I Will Bow; Through Human Hands
C The Word of the Lord; Body/Blood

Christmas

Holy Family
C Go Up with Joy; Enter with Thanks and Praise

Mary, Mother of God
Day of the Lord

Second Sunday after Christmas
Word of the Lord; Body/Blood

Epiphany
Walk Always; Rise Like Incense

Baptism of the Lord
Walk Always; Go, You Are Sent

Lent

First Sunday
A Let Your Spirit; Go Up with Joy
B Walk Always
C This Altar; Word of the Lord

Second Sunday
A Walk Always; Go, You Are Sent
B This Altar; Rise Like Incense
C Keeping Silence

Third Sunday
C Walk Always

Fourth Sunday
A Let Your Spirit; Through Human Hands

Fifth Sunday
C Go, You Are Sent

Passion Sunday
Take and Drink; Walk Always

Easter Season

Easter Sunday
Alleluia!

Second Sunday
A Sign of Peace; Through Human Hands

Third Sunday
A, B, C This Altar; We Bring You These Gifts; Bless Us, O Lord

Fourth Sunday
A I Am the Gate
C To Stand in Your Presence

Fifth Sunday
B I Will Bow

Sixth Sunday
A Through Human Hands
B Let Your Spirit; Through Human Hands
C A Sign of Peace; I Am the Gate; Enter with Thanks and Praise

Ascension of the Lord
To Stand in Your Presence; Rise Like Incense; Calling to Mind

Seventh Sunday
A Let Us Pray to the Lord; Let Your Spirit
C Word of the Lord; Go, You Are Sent

Pentecost
Go, You Are Sent; Let Your Spirit; A Sign of Peace

Trinity Sunday
I Will Bow

Corpus Christi
Body/Blood; We Bring You These Gifts

Ordinary Time

Second Sunday
A Through Human Hands
B Keeping Silence; Walk Always
C Singing in the Assembly

Third Sunday
A This Community Now Sends You Forth; Go, You Are Sent
B Walk Always; This Community Now Sends You Forth; Go, You Are Sent
C Word of the Lord; Through Human Hands

Fourth Sunday
A Go Up with Joy; We Bring You These Gifts
B Keeping Silence
C Word of the Lord

Fifth Sunday
A Go Up with Joy; Go, You Are Sent
B Go Up with Joy

Sixth Sunday
B Bless Us, O Lord; We Bring You These Gifts; Enter with Thanks and Praise
C Go Up with Joy

Seventh Sunday
C Let Your Spirit

Eighth Sunday
A Calling to Mind; Day of the Lord
B Keeping Silence
C Go Up with Joy

Ninth Sunday
A Word of the Lord
B Day of the Lord

Twelfth Sunday
B Keeping Silence

Fourteenth Sunday
B Through Human Hands
C Go Up with Joy; Go, You Are Sent

Fifteenth Sunday
A Word of the Lord
B This Community Now Sends You Forth; Go, You Are Sent
C Word of the Lord

Sixteenth Sunday
A Let Us Pray to the Lord
B Keeping Silence
C Enter with Thanks and Praise; Bless Us, O Lord

Seventeenth Sunday
B We Bring You These Gifts
C The Lifting Up of My Hands

Eighteenth Sunday
A Body/Blood
B Body/Blood
C Enter with Thanks and Praise

Nineteenth Sunday
A Keeping Silence
B We Bring You These Gifts; To Stand in Your Presence
C Walk Always

Twentieth Sunday
B Body/Blood; We Bring You These Gifts

Twenty-first Sunday
B Word of the Lord

Twenty-second Sunday
A Let Your Spirit; To Stand in Your Presence
B We Bring You These Gifts; Let Your Spirit
C Bless Us, O Lord; Take and Drink; Calling to Mind

Twenty-third Sunday
A Let Us Pray to the Lord
B Word of the Lord

Twenty-fourth Sunday
B Go, You Are Sent

Twenty-fifth Sunday
A Enter with Thanks and Praise; This Community Now Sends You Forth
C Go, You Are Sent; A Sign of Peace; Let Us Pray to the Lord

Twenty-sixth Sunday
B Through Human Hands

Twenty-seventh Sunday
A Let Us Pray to the Lord

Twenty-eighth Sunday
A Day of the Lord; Go Up with Joy; Enter with Thanks and Praise
B Singing in the Assembly (see the proper responsorial psalm)
C We Bring You These Gifts

Twenty-ninth Sunday
B Take and Drink
C Let Us Pray to the Lord

Thirtieth Sunday
A Go, You Are Sent
C I Will Bow

Thirty-first Sunday
A I Will Bow; Go, You Are Sent
C Enter with Thanks and Praise

Thirty-second Sunday
A Walk Always

Thirty-third Sunday
A Singing in the Assembly
B Take and Drink (see responsorial psalm)
C Singing in the Assembly (see responsorial psalm)

Christ the King Sunday
A Go, You are Sent; Day of the Lord
B Day of the Lord

C Day of the Lord; Enter with Thanks and Praise (see responsorial psalm)

2. With Other Rites

At Evening Prayer: Rise Like Incense

When the catechumens are dismissed: This Community Now Sends You Forth

When giving or receiving back the Lord's Prayer from the elect: The Lifting Up of My Hands

Dedication of a church/anniversary of dedication: This Altar; I Am the Gate

3. With Ministry Training

With all ministers: This Altar; I Will Bow; Day of the Lord; Keeping Silence; Singing in the Assembly; Go Up with Joy

With lectors: Word of the Lord

With eucharistic ministers: Body/Blood; We Bring You These Gifts; Calling to Mind; Let Your Spirit; Through Human Hands; To Stand in Your Presence; Take and Drink

With cantors, musicians, choir members: Singing in the Assembly; Alleluia!; Keeping Silence

With ushers: A Sign of Peace; Walk Always; Enter with Thanks and Praise